101
INSPIRING
STORIES

Principles for Successful Living

DR. G. FRANCIS XAVIER, PhD

JAICO PUBLISHING HOUSE

Ahmedabad Bangalore Bhopal Bhubaneswar Chennai
Delhi Hyderabad Kolkata Lucknow Mumbai

Published by Jaico Publishing House
A-2 Jash Chambers, 7-A Sir Phirozshah Mehta Road
Fort, Mumbai - 400 001
jaicopub@jaicobooks.com
www.jaicobooks.com

© Dr. G. Francis Xavier

101 INSPIRING STORIES
ISBN 978-81-8495-028-1

First Jaico Impression: 2009
Twelfth Jaico Impression: 2016

Printed by
Replika Press Pvt. Ltd.

Dedicated to
Rev. Fr. A.S. Antonisamy
with
Love and Respect

Contents

Foreword

All of us love stories. The fortunate among us grew up reading, listening, and enjoying many stories- the memories of which are fondly cherished for months, years and decades. These stories have enhanced our learning, enabled us to experience and enjoy the beautiful world around us as well as teach us many of the principles and truths that guide us in our wonderful journey called life. Stories have magical charm about them that appeal to the young and the young at heart.

Stories provide important insights that help us take on life's challenges in a proactive constructive manner. As time passes we are faced with never ending time challenges and this is where stories come to the rescue! Stories can be read in minutes, can change our state instantaneously, and can add to the quality of our lives in a heartbeat.

I met Dr. G Francis Xavier in Singapore and was immediately impressed with his energy, passion and enthusiasm. We discussed our normal mutual passion for learning, sharing and contribution to personal growth, self

development and personal awareness programme in India
and Singapore. One of the unique methodologies of training
that Dr. Francis Xavier adopts is "Story Meditation". He
has used hundreds of stories to accelerate learning and
accentuate the key messages in the stories. A few years
back the participants of his programmes urged him to
publish his stories. And I am pleased to add my support to
this wonderful initiative.

I am confident that this collection of marvelous stories
will provide insights to develop and explore one's identity.
These stories will inspire, entertain, educate and bring a
smile to the reader's face! As stories appeal to all people,
we can use these wonderful stories as tools of learning,
teaching, sharing and connecting with friends, family,
colleagues, associates and our inner self.

Happy story reading, story sharing and story telling!

—Dave Rogers,
Director Competitive Edge
Singapore

Preface

I am a voracious reader and particularly love reading books on self-improvement. This I do with great passion to improve my own personality. A pursuit that is going strong for over four decades!

I have collected thousands of inspiring stories that are used in my training programme called "TAP YOUR GENIUS". This is a technique-oriented multidimensional Personality Development Programme designed to ignite the spark of genius in the participants. Relevant to the topic on hand I tell a story impregnated with the philosophy, principle and practice of self-improvement. The end of the story is not revealed and the participants are urged to come up with their own answers. I call this process "Story Meditation".

My participants enjoy these stories. At their insistence I wrote THE WORLD'S BEST INSPIRING STORIES, which was well received by thousands around the country.

This book 101 Inspiring Stories also contains stories that

have been carefully chosen. I have included in this only those stories that inspired me the most. They are drawn from various sources. My contribution is the language and the explanation of the implication of each story.

To get Maximum Benefit from this Book: Go through the story. Reflect for a moment on the two questions at the end. Think of the possible answers. Then refer to the answers given. If you follow this procedure, your creativity will improve and you will get the maximum out of this book.

Parents, present this book to your children. They would not just love these stories, their personality too will improve to a considerable extent without your 'sermon'.

—Dr. G. Francis Xavier Ph. D.
358, 8th Main, Viveknagar
Bangalore-560047
Mob. 09449544358 / 09343721820
E-Mail: gfrancisxavier@yahoo.co.in

Acknowledgement

I owe a deep sense of gratitude to all those who have been a source of inspiration and encouragement in my literary pursuit.

I sincerely thank Mr. Dave Rogers, Chief Coach and Director of Competitive Edge, Singapore, for writing an appropriate Foreword for this book.

I am extremely thankful to Mr. Akash Shah, the Publisher, Mr. R.H. Sharma, the Chief Editor of Jaico Publishing House, Mumbai for publishing this book in an excellent manner.

In addition I wish to acknowledge with deep sense of gratitude, all my friends and participants of my various training programmes. The number is too large to mention. However, the following persons deserve special mention. The names are given in an alphabetical order for easy reference.

V. Acharya, Amudha P. Kandasamy, Arpudamary, Arulmarianathan, Babu K., Verghese, Bharat Kapasi, Bishop

Joseph D'Silva (late), Bro. Jacob Ezhanikat, R. Devaraj, Elgy Danny, Emmanual Das, Ethirajulu Naidu, P. Gasper, K.J. George, Fr. Giri Raju, Giri Rao, Gunakodi Sekar, Ilyas Montri, Indrajeet Singh, Jacob Abraham, Jaiprakash Tiwari, Fr. Jayanathan, John Joseph, Dr. M Joseph, I Joseph Victor, K. Jothiramalingam, Mrs. Kalpa Rajesh, M. Kandasamy, R. Kantharaj, Krishna Kishore, M. Kuruvan, Madhu, Malathi Gerard, V Manikesi, M.S. Manjunath, Mary Okelo, M.B. Meti, Dr. K. Nakkiran, K.K. Namboodri, O.P. Narang, P. Narayana Bhat, Sr. Nicola Sprenger, Nigel Fernandes, Patrick D'Souza, Dr. Pius K. Okela (late), Fr. Pradeep Sequira, Prahalad N. Kalra, Prakash Gangaram, Quadsia Gandhi, Radhakrishnan, Rajesh K. Padia, Rajiv Beri, E. Ravichandran, J.N. Reddy, Reinhard Sprenger, Fr. Ronnie Prabhu, Mrs. Shaila George, Shankar Bhavsar, Shanmugha Verma, Simen Lourds, Stanlay Karkada, Steven Pinto, R. Sundar Raj, Sunil Raval, D. Thankaraj, M.V.M. Velmurugan, M. Vijaya Kumar, Vincent A. Pinto, Yesudasan Mories.

I am highly indebted to my family members for their unstinted support and cooperation in my literary pursuit: My wife A. Antoniammal, my children and their spouses, Dr. Denis, Freeda, Prakash, Rupa, Sheela, Peter and my grandchildren Nikita, Alan, Preethika, and Rosanna.

—Dr. G. Francis Xavier Ph. D.

I
Captivate the Heart of Your Enemy

Ahighly successful grocer had a well-furnished shop. He had a flourishing business. The grocer was naturally happy that many customers patronized him, and regularly came to his shop for their daily requirements. To his utter shock and disappointment a large departmental store was constructed just in front of his shop. The grocer thought that the departmental store would drive him out of business. With great distress he approached the Master and told him that his family had owned his shop for a century. To lose it now would be his undoing, for there was nothing else he was skilled at.

The Master said: "If you fear the owner of the departmental store, you will hate him. And hatred will be your downfall."

"What should I do then?" asked the distraught grocer.

"Each morning walk out of your shop onto the sidewalk and bless your shop, wishing it prosperity. Then turn to face the departmental store and bless it too."

"What? Bless my competitor and destroyer?"

"Any blessing you give him will rebound to your good. Any
evil you wish him will destroy you."

After a year the grocer came to the Master to inform him
that he had to close down his shop as he feared.

■ QUESTIONS

1. Why did the grocer close down his shop?

2. What is the implication of this story?

Check our answers only after you have tried to come up
with your own.

■ ANSWERS

1. Since he became the owner of the departmental store
   he had to close down his grocery shop.

2. We do not live in isolation. Every element in the universe
   is woven together. This is a scientific truth. Our
   thoughts have the potential to travel across multidimensional planes. Every feeling that we experience or
   entertain pervades the entire universe. The good
   thoughts that we have about a person reach him
   unconsciously. Every person can (in some way or the
   other) sense the good or bad feeling of others. This is
   an inevitable phenomenon happening continuously in
   our life, with or without our conscious knowledge. Since

the grocer did not hate the owner of the departmental store, but rather blessed his store; in due course, they became good friends and the grocer had become a partner in the departmental store. Since the grocer had more experience, he could run the departmental store more efficiently. Ultimately, the earlier owner sold all his rights of the departmental store to the grocer, and left the town for good.

2

The difference between Learning and Wisdom

A company once recruited two employees, equally competent and intelligent, but from different backgrounds. While employee A was stylish, confident, and had graduated from the country's best institution, employee B was rather subdued yet sophisticated, with no great qualifications to boast of other than a few years of experience. However, employee B was always considered the wiser of the two and often given better opportunities. Employee A was upset and asked the President of the company why he was considered less wise, when he was definitely more learned than B. The President's answer made A understand the real perspective of life.

■ QUESTIONS

1. What was the President's answer?

2. What is the implication of this story?

■ ANSWERS

1. The President said, "Learning is acquired by reading books or listening to lectures. Wisdom is acquired by reading the book that is you."

2. Acquiring knowledge by reading books and listening to lectures is passive and external. This is only borrowed stuff. "Reading the book that is you" involves the process of thinking, imagining, visualizing, deciding, etc. These processes are active and internal. They are original and creative. The world has been able to make scientific and technological progress only through the efforts of the people who could visualize and imagine. Imagination is more powerful than mere knowledge. Wisdom emerges out of self-knowledge. 'Reading the book that is you' is not an easy task at all, for every minute of the day brings a new edition of the book.

3

Reach the Land of Laughter

The Master was in an expansive mood, so his disciples sought to learn from him the stages he had passed through in his quest for the divine. "God first led me by the hand," he said, "into the land of action and there I dwelt for several years. He returned and led me to the land of sorrow where I lived until my heart was purged of every inordinate attachment. That is when I found myself in the hand of love whose burning flames consumed whatever was left in me of the Self. Then he took me to the land of silence where the mysteries of life and death revealed themselves before my wondering eyes,"

"Was that the final stage of your quest?" they asked.

"No," said the Master, and continued...

■ QUESTIONS

1. What did the Master further say to his disciples?

2. What is the implication of this story?

■ ANSWERS

1. "One day God said, "Today I shall take you to the innermost sanctuary of the temple, to the heart of God himself,' and I was led to the Land of Laughter."

2. When you laugh, you are happy. When you are happy you can't have the feeling of hatred, resentment, jealously and other negative emotions. In the absence of negative emotions, there is love and compassion. This is the last stage of spirituality. This is easily brought by anyone just by laughing, laughing and laughing.

4
Understand Passion with Compassion

An old woman in China supported a monk for more than twenty years. She built him a little hut, and fed him while he spent all his time in meditation.

At the end of this period, she wondered what progress the man had made. She decided to put him to test by enlisting the help of a girl aflame with desire. "Go into the hut, and embrace him," she told the girl. The girl called on the monk that night, only to find him meditating. Without further ado she began to caress him and said, "What are we going to do now?" The monk got into a towering rage at this impertinence, and took a broom and drove the girl out of the hut.

The girl got back and reported to the old woman.

■ QUESTIONS

1. What was the reaction of the old woman?

2. What is the implication of this story?

■ ANSWERS

1. When she got back and reported what had happened, the old woman was indignant. "To think that I fed that fellow for twenty years," she exclaimed. "He showed no understanding of your need, no disposition to guide you in your error. He need not have given in to your passion, but after all these years of prayer he could at least have developed some compassion after doing so many years of sadhana.

2. Sadhana (exalted achievement) and tapas (austerities) are expected to be done for self-purification and not for self-glorification. A self-purified person would have understood the passion of the woman in our story. The mere fact that the monk got angry with the woman shows that he had been doing this for his self-glorification. There is an element of too much ego in his action. A person of prayer and meditation should never get angry with anyone for any reason.

5

Do Miracles in Your Life

V. Beckman once went out for a picnic with his family. His car was parked in a slope. His four-year-old son was playing close to the car. All of a sudden, the car started moving and his son was practically about to be caught under the wheel. Seeing this, Beckman grabbed the bumper of the heavy car and tried to lift it to save his son.

■ QUESTIONS

1. Was he able to save his son?

2. What is the implication of this story?

■ ANSWERS

1. Beckman lifted the car miraculously high enough to save his son from the tragedy of being crushed under the wheel.

2. In this context let me quote the story related by, Swami Chinmayananda in his book Life and Meditation.

"Now think: suddenly you hear that your house is on fire. You rush therein and find that the entire house is in flames, and the fire brigade is standing helpless. At that time you find your wife walking out of the fire with a child in hand. When you make enquiries, you hear spellbound the thrilling news that the child was sleeping upstairs in a room. In the panic, everybody ran helter-skelter, and then the mother remembered the child. The fire man, in spite of his forty years of experience, said, "Maa, no human being can go therein. The whole thing is ablaze. "The mother immediately forgets everything and in a hysterical ecstasy she runs into the fire. Everybody is expecting that she would come out like a 'Pakora'. Instead, they find that not even her saree has been burnt. She rushes to the room, takes the child and comes out. After this incident, tell her to go near the fire, and she is afraid, her efficiency has gone. But, under the inspiration of that great love for her child, she could do miracles. If that is the potentiality of the human mind, can't she live twenty-four hours of the day as a heroine? She cannot, because she has not got that inspiring goal. So an ordinary man may be a coward, but when he is inspired by a great ideal, you will find that, out of himself he pulls out miraculously a new stream of energy and vitality."

6

How to Solve Marital Problems

Amarriage counselor was once questioned about the problems between husband and wife, and the ways to solve them. The following is the text of his narration; "Sometimes, when a husband and wife come to me complaining bitterly about their marriage partner, I ask them to write opposite each accusation, the quality that they once admired, or still admire. But, I've never yet encountered a case where the complainant was unable to find something complimentary about that particular characteristic. Very often this simple devise proves to be a turning point in the whole relationship. One man to whom I gave this advice carried it a step further. That evening at home, he sat down near his wife with a pad and a pencil, looked at her speculatively from time to time and began to write. 'What are you doing?,' she finally asked him. 'Writing a list of your good qualities'. 'Good qualities?,' she echoed incredulously. 'I didn't know you thought I had any'. 'Well you do,' he said, and went on writing. Out of curiosity she wanted to see what he had written, so she asked him to show. He demurred, but finally yielded. She read what he had written with amazement and pleasure. 'Why?" she said, 'I had no idea that anything about me, pleased you anymore.' 'Lots of things do, a few don't', he said cheerfully. 'Well,' she said, 'While you are at it you'd better list those too'. 'I will,' he said, 'if you do the same for me.'

■ QUESTIONS

1. What was the result of this exercise?

2. What is the implication of this story?

■ ANSWERS

1. The upshot was that both of them got their grievances out in the open in such a calm and amicable way that they were able to resolve quite a few of them.

2. Martial problems arise mostly due to non-communication. When married partners start communicating their feelings towards each other honestly all problems can be easily solved.

7
Penitence is Better Than Pride

There is a story of an oriental sultan who regularly got up early in the morning to pray. One day, he failed to wake up at the hour of the prayer. The devil woke him up that morning and told him to get up and pray. "Who are you?" the sultan asked. "Never mind who I am as long as my act is good." "Yes, but I think you are Satan and you must have some bad motive. I just wish to know why you wanted me to get up and pray." Well,' said the devil....

■ QUESTIONS

1. What did the devil say to the sultan?

2. What is the implication of this story?

■ ANSWERS

1. "If you had slept and forgotten your prayers, you would be sorry for it afterwards, and such kind of penitence would be more pleasing to God. But if you go on as

now, and do not neglect a single prayer for ten years, you will be so satisfied with yourself and may fall into a deadly sin of pride and that would be more pleasing to me." Said the Satan.

2. Fault mixed with penitence is better than virtue mixed with pride.

8

The Essence of Religion in One Word

A Governor was once on his regular travelling spree. He stepped in to pay homage to the great Master on his way. "Affairs of the state leave me no time for lengthy dissertations. Could you put the essence of religion into one paragraph or two for a busy man like me?"

The Master replied, "I can put it into a single word for the benefit of your Highness."

"Incredible! What is that unusual word?," asked the Governor.

"Silence," said the Master.

"And what is the way to silence?"

"Meditation"

"And what, may I ask, is meditation?"

The Master answered.......

■ QUESTIONS

1. What did the Master answer?

2. What is the implication of the Story?

■ ANSWERS

1. The Master answered again, "Silence."

2. Silence here means inner and outer silence. Normally, people maintain outer silence in meditation. Outer silence comes when a person does not communicate with others, either orally or in writing. The most important thing in meditation is to have inner silence. In the mind, there is a continuous inner dialogue going on day in and day out. The purpose of meditation is to stop the inner dialogue of the mind. The contents of the inner dialogue would be either the past or the future. Meditation is the shutting out, for a given period of time each day, the many things which make a constant demand on everyone. It is the stilling of the mind (silence) to the hue and cry of the everyday world.

9

Thinking is Superior to Doing

An efficiency expert at Ford Motors was once making his report to Henry Ford. "As you will see, Sir, the report is highly favourable, except for that man down the hall. Every time I pass by, he's sitting with his feet on his desk. He's wasting your money."

Henry Ford merely smiled, and said something which was a lesson for the expert.

■ QUESTIONS

1. What did Henry Ford tell him?

2. What is the implication of this story?

■ ANSWERS

1. Said Ford — "That same man once had an idea that earned us a fortune. At the time, I believe his feet were exactly where they are now."

2. Whatever we see on this planet is the creation of the

thinking mind. It is thinking and imagination that makes the world what it is now. The modern dictum is "work smarter, not harder." If you want to work smarter, use the faculty of thinking. Very few people think. Only those who think produce results.

IO
Always React Positively

There was once a priest so holy that he never thought ill of anyone. One day, he sat down at a restaurant for a cup of coffee; which was all he could take, it being a day of fast and abstinence. When to his surprise, he saw a young member of his congregation devouring a massive steak at the next table. "I trust I haven't shocked you, Father," said the young fellow with a smile, "Ah! I take it that you forgot that today is a day of fast and abstinence," said the priest.

"No, I remember it very clearly."

"Then you must be sick, and the doctor must have forbidden you to fast."

"Not at all, I am in the best of my health."

At that the priest raised his eyes heavenwards and said something which shamed the young fellow.

■ QUESTIONS

1. What did the priest say?

2. What is the implication of this story?

■ ANSWERS

1. The priest said to God. "What an example this younger generation is to us. Isn't it great that they admit their sins than lie?"

2. The holier we are the greater the possibility to look at everything positively. A variety of stimuli are presented to us daily. If we react positively, we develop a positive personality. On the other hand, negative reactions would land us into several problems. The world looks green to an optimist, and black to the pessimist.

11

Lose Yourself in the Service of Others

Some years ago, a rabbi used to disappear each week on the eve of the Sabbath. His congregation grew suspicious of his unusual disappearance. They decided to investigate. They deputed one of their members to follow him. Their suspicion was that he might be meeting the Almighty secretly. This is what the man saw. The rabbi disguised himself in peasant clothes and served a paralyzed gentile woman (low-caste woman) in her cottage, cleaning up the room and preparing a Sabbath meal for her.

When the spy got back to the congregation, he was questioned, 'So, where did the rabbi go? Did he ascend to Heaven?"

■ QUESTION

1. What did the spy reply?

2. What is the implication of this story?

■ ANSWERS

1. The spy replied, "No, even higher than Heaven."

2. Lose your life in the service of others. It is far better
   and superior than even going to heaven. In this context,
   the poem of Ralph Waldo Trine is pertinent to quote:

   "Are you seeking for greatness, O brother of mine,

   As the full, fleeting seasons and years glide away

   If seeking directly and for self alone.

   The true and abiding you can never say.

   But all self-forgetting, know well the law,

   It's the hero, and not the self-seeker, who is crowned

   Then go lose your life in the service of others

   And lo! With rare greatness and glory it will abound

   You will reach higher than heaven."

12

Children can be Smarter

A woman was holding a religious function at her place, and had prepared lots of laddoos for the occasion. Her son, a regular brat, used to steal sweets from the kitchen. On this occasion, the mother caught him in the act, and pulled him next to God's statue and questioned him. "Did you know that God was present when you stole that laddoo?"

"Yes", the boy replied.

"And he was looking at you all the time?"

"Yes", said the boy again.

"And what do you think he was saying to you?"

The boy gave an answer that left his mother absolutely in splits.

■ QUESTIONS

1. What was the boy's reply?

2. What is the implication of this story?

■ ANSWERS

1. The boy said, "God was saying, there's no one here but
    the two of us, so take two laddoos."

2. You may enjoy the humour here. But the profound
    truth is that we have not seen God. It is only a concept
    in our mind. Children believe what they can see or hear.
    They can't go beyond what is practically present. To
    speak to them about the demon, to frighten them not
    to do something or to do something, is the same as
    telling them about God for similar reasons. It is better
    not to talk about God or Demon when they are too
    small to understand.

13
Motivate to do something

There was a French bishop who was a gifted orator. He was once asked what he considered his greatest compliment.

The bishop replied, "My greatest compliment is not when people come up to me and say – 'What a great sermon you gave, what a wonderful preacher you are. But…."

◼ QUESTIONS

1. What did the Bishop further say?

2. What is the implication of this story?

◼ ANSWERS

1. The Bishop said: "The greatest compliment is when someone comes to me and says that he was motivated to do something after hearing my sermon."

2. The main objective of giving a sermon in a church service is to motivate people to be good, and also to do only good. Action speaks much louder than all the words in the Holy Scriptures on this planet. If this does not happen, the entire sermon becomes a ritual.

14

Prepare well for a Glorious Old Age

A Swiss journalist, who had worked hard all his life and earned a lot of fame and money because of his good work, decided to retire. His last interview was to be with the new Italian Prime Minister, Alciude de Gaspari. After the interview was over, and both of them settled down for some tea and informal talk, the journalist casually remarked, "This is my last interview, I am 65 and about to retire."

The new Prime Minister commented:

■ QUESTIONS

1. What was the comment of the new Prime Minister?

2. What is the implication of this story?

■ ANSWERS

1. The Prime Minister remarked, "Oh! What a pity, I am 65 too, but on the threshold of a new career."

2. Age is no bar to start a new career. There are many
   instances in history when people started late and attained
   remarkable achievements. Srila Prabhupada, founder of
   the worldwide movement Krishna Consciousness, is one
   such individual. At 69, he went to the United States
   from India. Before leaving India, he had written three
   books. In the next twelve years, he wrote more than
   sixty. Before he left India, he had initiated one disciple.
   In the next twelve years, he initiated more than four
   thousand. Before sailing for America, he had never been
   outside India. But in the next twelve years, he traveled
   many times around the world propagating the Krishna
   Consciousness movement.

Note this: Although his life contribution may appear to
have come in a late burst of revolutionary spiritual
achievements, the first sixty-nine years of his life were a
preparation for what he achieved in his life time.

15
Liberate Yourself by Forgiving

It is often said that friends in troubled times are friends forever. A former inmate of a Nazi concentration camp had come to meet his friend, who had undergone the same ordeal with him years before. After the exchange of the usual pleasantries, both of them got talking about their personal lives, and one of them exclaimed, "Well, I haven't really gotten over the whole thing, I am still consumed with so much hatred for the Nazis."

■ QUESTIONS

1. What did the other say to this?

2. What is the implication of this story?

■ ANSWERS

1. Well", the other friend said, "they still have you in the prison."

2. Hatred brings bondage. Forgiveness liberates. Once the enemies are forgiven we have peace of mind, and we are at liberty to function at our optimum level. Hatred causes stress and tension, which bring down our productivity.

16

Make Perseverance your Bosom Friend

Gilbert Becker was a God-loving soldier who once made a pilgrimage to the Holy Land. As destiny would have it, he was taken prisoner by a Saracen, and was kept in hiding for days on end. This Saracen had a lovely daughter who fell in love with Gilbert, and with her help, he escaped back to London. But she couldn't forget Gilbert. One night, she left her father's place to find her lost love in London. She was a stranger to the place, and could not speak a word of English. To top it all, she did not have Gilbert's address. Determined though sad, she cried and roamed the streets calling out his name – Gilbert... Gilbert... Gilbert... Gilbert. Days and months passed, but her search gave no results. She still persisted, more determined than before. Slowly, the word spread around in the city and reached Gilbert's ears. On hearing this Gilbert....

■ QUESTIONS

1. What do you think Gilbert did?

2. What is the implication of this story?

■ ANSWERS

1. He was genuinely touched by her love for him, and married her.

2. Her perseverance is laudable. Through perseverance, you can achieve almost anything. By trying again and again, even the most stubborn vice can be removed and virtues can be developed. If you try again and again, nothing is impossible for you to achieve. This virtue of perseverance is one of the hallmarks of all great achievers on this planet. "If you wish success in life, make perseverance your bosom friend, experience your counselor, accept caution as your elder brother, and hope as your guardian angel."

(Joseph Addison)

17

Be Courteous – Win the Heart of Others

President Lincoln was known the world over for his courteous and hospitable nature. He never discriminated between people. Once, while strolling with an officer, he met a black beggar who greeted him respectfully. The President, in turn, tipped his hat to the beggar. The official asked Lincoln in surprise: "Why did you tip your hat to the uncouth beggar? To this, the President replied with a smile…

■ QUESTIONS

1. What was the President's reply?

2. What is the implication of this story?

■ ANSWERS

1. The President replied, "I have never wanted anyone to be more courteous than I am."

2. Courtesy wins the heart of all. Courtesy blossoms where there is humility. Humility is the hallmark of saints. One should practice this virtue of courtesy in one's day-to-day life.

18

Give while you are Alive

A pig constantly lamented his lack of popularity. He would always go up to his friend cow, and complain that people were always speaking so well of the cow but no one ever had a good word for him. True, the cow gave milk and cream, but he maintained that pigs gave even more, they provided man with bacon, ham and bristles for brushes. He demanded to know the reason for such lack of appreciation. The cow thought for a while, and then remarked...

■ QUESTIONS

1. What was the cow's remark?

2. What is the implication of this story?

■ ANSWERS

1. The cow replied, "May be it is because I give while I am alive whereas you give only after you are dead."

2. Some people accumulate wealth without enjoying a bit

of what they have earned. They save for the future and for old age. Death being uncertain, it may take anyone by surprise. In such an event, the amount so accumulated would be of no avail to the person who greedily saved without spending. It is better to spend and also give as much as possible for charity. Derive happiness in giving while you are alive.

19
Be firm in your Conviction

One Saturday, Mr. Girard, an atheist millionaire of Philadelphia, ordered all his clerks to come to the office the next day and help unload the newly arrived order.

One young man replied quietly, "Mr. Girard, I cannot work on Sundays," "You know the rules, young man?" asked Mr. Girard.

"Yes, I know, but I cannot work on Sundays."

"Well, then step up to the desk and the cashier will settle your accounts for good ."

One day, a banker came to Girard and asked him to recommend a man for the post of a new cashier at his bank. Girard strongly recommended a person for the post.

■ QUESTIONS

1. Whom did Girard recommend for the post of a cashier in the bank?

2. What is the implication of this story?

■ ANSWERS

1. Girard recommended strongly the dismissed young man for the post of a cashier in the bank.

2. Although Girard dismissed the man, he recognized his sterling character. Anyone who would sacrifice his own interests for what he believed to be right would make a loyal, trustworthy cashier.

20

Abandon Everything for Spiritual Growth

There was once a very sincere disciple named Sumedh, who tried very hard to understand the meaning of spirituality. He read books, travelled far and wide, enrolled himself for a number of meditation courses, but his efforts resulted in no good. Finally, he joined the Master at his monastery, and every month, Sumedh would faithfully send his Master an account of his spiritual progress. In the first month, he wrote, "I feel an expansion of consciousness and experience my oneness with the universe." The Master threw the note away. The second month, he wrote, "I have finally discovered that the disciple is present in all things." The Master was terribly disappointed. The third month, he wrote, "The mystery of the one and the many has been revealed to my wondering gaze." The Master yawned. In the next month's report he wrote, "No one is born, no one lives, and no one dies." The Master threw up his hands in despair.

After that, the Master didn't hear from him for over a year, and finally the Master reminded him of his monthly notes. This time he wrote something that made the Master jump with joy.

■ QUESTIONS

1. What did Sumedh write?

2. What is the implication of this story?

■ ANSWERS

1. He wrote: "Who cares?"

2. Spiritual advancement is measured not in terms of what you learn or what you innovate, but how far you can renounce and abandon the worldly pleasures and expectations.

21

There is so much to Explore in Nature

APProtestant Bishop once paid an annual visit to one of the schools run by his Church. Since he had come there after a long time, he decided to stay overnight. After dinner, he had a chat with the Principal of the school. During discussion, the Bishop said, "Man has unravelled the mysteries of Nature, and has indeed discovered many things that proved to be useful to society. But I don't think that he can explore any further. I strongly feel that the world would come to an end soon."

The Principal disagreed, "Man is still in the process of discovering more and more. Within fifty years, man will be capable of inventing many more things on this planet."

"Can you mention at least one?" challenged the Bishop.

"Why, man might soon learn to fly," said the Principal.

"Rubbish!" said the Bishop, "If God intended man to fly, he would have surely given him wings. But he gave these only to birds and insects, because he wanted them and not man to fly."

■ QUESTIONS

1. Do you know the name of the Bishop?

2. What is the implication of this story?

■ ANSWERS

1. The Bishop's name was Wright. He had two sons named Orville and Wilbur. They went on to make history by inventing the aeroplane.

2. Only through optimism and vision can technological innovations be possible. One must believe that there is so much on this planet to unravel. Through constant research and hard work, man can surely be capable of exploring nature in a better way, and inventions would follow one after another. He must however, use these inventions and discoveries to make life more meaningful for every single being on this planet.

22
Speak Kindly

A convict from Darlington, England was released from jail after serving three years for embezzlement.

One day, he happened to pass Mayor John Morel on the streets. Embarrassed and completely withdrawn due to what he had done earlier, the convict could not face the Mayor and pretended not to see him at all. He hurriedly walked past the Mayor. But all of a sudden, he felt a warm hand hold his trembling one. The Mayor spoke in a loving and compassionate tone, "Hello! I am so glad to see you! How are you?" The man was still unable to come to terms with what had just happened, and their meeting ended quite abruptly.

Years later, according to the story told by J.H. Jowett, Morel accidentally met the same man in another town. This time the young man was a reformed person altogether. He stopped the Mayor himself, looked into his eyes and said, "Sir, I want to thank you for whatever you did for me when I came out of the prison." "What did I do?" asked the Mayor, surprised.

■ QUESTIONS

1. What was the convict's reply?

2. What is the implication of this story?

■ ANSWERS

1. "When the world turned its back on me for a crime I committed, you accepted me as a human being first. When I had no one to call my own, you held out your hand to me. Whatever I am today, it is because of that day, when you spoke a kind word to me. It has surely changed my life and I have none other than you to be grateful to," replied the man.

2. A kind word, a compassionate hug and a smile can change someone's life forever and make a big difference. We have the power to make such a difference in someone's life. Let us pledge to use this power as often as we possibly can.

23
Don't be Stupidly Frugal

❦

A man was once brought before the judge for taking a bribe. The judge offered him a choice of punishments to choose from – eat 5 kilos of onions, be given 50 lashes, or pay a thousand rupees. The greedy convict did not want to part with his money, so he refused to take that option. If he opted for the fifty lashes, he was sure to die before they even got over. So, he volunteered to eat the onions. He couldn't eat more than a couple and had to give up that option too. As for the lashes, the excruciating pain he underwent by the time he reached ten lashes was enough for him to scream, "Spare me please, I will pay the money, much more if you so wish!" Thus, the foolish man ended up getting a taste of all three punishments simply because he wanted to save a few bucks.

■ QUESTIONS

1. What is the implication of this story?

■ ANSWERS

1. Many people give too much importance to money and neglect other aspects of life. Money is not everything in life. Money can buy you pleasure, but it can't buy happiness. Money can take you to a beauty salon, but it can't make you beautiful. It can buy medicine, but it can't give you perfect health. It can buy you all the gymnastic equipments, but it can't give you good physique. You may be able to afford a good coffin, but it can't make sure that you'll have a good and peaceful death.

24

Trust in God but do your best

There was once a priest sitting at his desk by the window composing a sermon on providence, when he heard something that sounded like an explosion. Soon, there were people running to and fro in panic. It so happened that a dam had burst, and the river gushed into the village in full spate. Naturally, the people were being evacuated. The priest saw the water begin to rise in the street below. After all, he too was a human, and felt panic rising inside him. But then he thought, "Here I am preparing a sermon on providence. Perhaps God Almighty wants to test my faith in him. He has given me the opportunity to practice what I preach. I shall not flee like everyone else, but stay right here trusting in the providence of God to save me."

By this time, the water had reached almost up to the windows. A boat-full of people came. "Jump in Father," they shouted.

"Ah no, my children,' said Father confidently, "I trust in the providence of God to save me." The priest frantically climbed onto the roof of his house. It did not take long for the water to reach the top. Another boatload of people went by urging Father to join them. Again he refused.

When the water came up to his knees, an officer in a motor boat was sent to rescue him. "No, thank you, Officer, said Father, with a smile. "I trust in God. You see, he will never let me down."

Ultimately, the Father drowned and went to Heaven. The first thing he did was to complain to God. "I trusted you! Why did you do nothing to save me?"

"Well," God said.

■ QUESTIONS

1. What did God say to the priest?

2. What is the implication of this story?

■ ANSWERS

1. "I did send three boats, you know."

2. It is indeed foolish to believe that God would come to our rescue every now and then. We have to take it upon ourselves to try and save our own life. And God will do the rest. We ought to believe in cause and effect. Trust in God, and do our best as per the given circumstances. As they say, "GOD HELPS THOSE WHO HELP THEMSELVES."

25
Captivate Hearts through Humour

President Roosevelt was asked, in a press conference, to relate the most interesting incident of his life. President Roosevelt often enjoyed relating this particular anecdote. It so happened that when the President was the Police Commissioner of New York, he was asked to interview an Irish applicant for the police force. Roosevelt asked the applicant what he would do to disperse a rioting mob. The applicant's prompt reply not only got him a place in the force, but won him appreciation for his quick wit.

■ QUESTIONS

1. What was the applicant's reply?

2. What is the implication of this story?

■ ANSWERS

1. The applicant's reply was, "I would pass my hat around for a collection."

2. A sense of humour makes life worth living. You can bring people closer if you can learn to make someone laugh.

26

Scientific Research too is a Form of Prayer

Once Pierre Curie, the great French scientist, was sitting in his laboratory with his head bowed down on a microscope. It almost looked as if he was praying. At that moment, one of his students entered the lab to meet him. Thinking that he was praying, the student was quietly leaving the lab. Just then, Curie lifted his head and called out to the student. The student told him: "Sir, since you were praying I did not want to disturb you."

The great scientist replied:

■ QUESTIONS

1. What was the scientist's reply?

2. What is the implication of this story?

■ ANSWERS

1. The scientist replied: "My dear boy, isn't work a form
   of worship? It is only through this prayer that we walk
   on the path towards Him. Through these, God reveals
   his eternal truths. When we do our research reverently,
   we stumble upon the many mysteries of God."

2. The world is shrouded in wonders and mysteries.
   Through scientific research, many mysteries of the world
   are unravelled, thus taking mankind a step further.

27

Develop the virtue of Patience

Sir Isaac Newton had an adorable but a very mischievous dog named Diamond. One night, when Newton wasn't at home, Diamond knocked over a candle which set fire to the book on his desk, and soon the book was turned into a half-burnt pile of papers. This book was the result of eight whole years of hard work and efforts. But when Newton came back home and saw the catastrophe, his reaction to this accident was ....

■ QUESTIONS

1. What was Newton's reaction?

2. What is the implication of this story?

■ ANSWERS

1. Sir Isaac Newton called Diamond by his side and said, "Diamond, little do you know the trouble and labour to which you have put your Master." Then he did not look upon that great work as lost forever like most

people would have done. He sat down at his desk to start all over again.

2. Patience is the key to success. A person who gets emotionally agitated becomes incapable of understanding things in the right perspective. On the other hand, a person of substance holds control of his/her emotional life, and is therefore able to use his/her intelligence to the highest degree. Such a person remains calm even in difficult situations and is not easily provoked. That is why he/she is able to coordinate his/her ideal with concrete reality.

28

Learn the Secret of Amassing Wealth

There was once a rich farmer who owned many acres of land, and had plenty of money in the bank too. With sheer hard work and determination, the farmer had earned enormous wealth during the span of his life. He was well-known as a source of inspiration to many. A journalist once approached him with the idea of doing a feature on him in the newspaper. "Sir, we would like to know the secret to such name and fame. But first, can you tell our readers, how exactly did you earn so much money?"

It did not take the farmer more than one sentence to explain his secret to the eager journalist.

■ QUESTIONS

1. What was the farmer's reply?

2. What is the implication of this story?

■ ANSWERS

1. "It's really a long story. Let us settle down a little first. Why don't you put off the light, so that we can save some electricity?" said the farmer.

2. Those who earn wealth through their efforts and hard work value every bit of what they earn. They save each and every paisa of what they earn. They are very meticulous about their savings, and make sure they do not waste anything. Whatever is saved is again ploughed back into their business, and thus it grows bigger and better.

29
What is Silence?

There was once a very famous monastery on the outskirts of a village. The chief of the monastery was well known for his knowledge and wisdom. Thanks to his popularity, people thronged to the monastery to pay their respects to the revered chief. Unfortunately, due to this crowd, the peace and calm of the monastery was totally shattered. The disciples were troubled, but the Master was as content with the noise as he was with the silence.

To his protesting disciples, the Master once said...

■ QUESTIONS

1. What did the Master say to his disciples?

2. What is the implication of this story?

■ ANSWERS

1. "Silence is not the absence of sound, but the absence of Self," said the Master.

2. 'Self' here refers to one's own personal sense of existence. It is the agenda of what had been thought, felt, and done during one's life time. The personal entity of a person is his Self. It includes one's problems, anguish, happiness, sorrow, etc. But one must remember that a meditative state is achieved not by anything else, but by learning to set aside the Self. It is almost like stepping out of one's garments and sitting calmly. It is a mind devoid of thoughts, aspirations and desires. Silence can be obtained when there is no thought — not of the world, not even of the Self.

30
Stick to Your Principles

The father of the nation, Mahatma Gandhi, was once invited to the Round Table Conference held in Britain way back in 1931. The Mahatma wore his usual loin cloth and attended the conference. The members were shocked to see this kind of attire, and there was a huge hue and cry made about it. Mahatma Gandhi was ridiculed, mocked and insulted by the British people, but it simply did not deter his self-confidence and calm demeanour. At the press conference, the British journalists were simply waiting to bombard him with questions about it. But, the answer they got was surely not going to be forgotten by them for a long time to come. What's more, it was splashed in the front page of every leading national daily the next day.

■ QUESTIONS

1. What was Gandhiji's reply when questioned about his dress?

2. What is the implication of this story?

■ ANSWERS

1. Gandhiji merely said, "You wear plus Four and I wear Minus Four!"

2. Gandhiji's firmness not to relinquish his principles for the sake of social etiquette was simply unbeatable. His answer meant to show to the world that he was not going to be dictated about how he should dress up. The way in which he gave this answer showed his sense of humour and discretion.

31

Be totally absorbed in whatever you do

There was a famous Hindi writer by the name of Suryakant Thripathi. He was popularly known as 'Nirala' because all his writings were under the pen name of Nirala.

Nirala enjoyed playing with children. One day he was playing with children on the streets. Some people who had not seen him earlier came to visit Nirala and asked Nirala himself: "Would you kindly show us the house of Nirala? We have come to visit him." Nirala told them, "Please wait for a while. I shall show his house a little later." He continued his play, and after finishing he informed them that he was Nirala. The visitors were surprised and asked him. "Why did you not inform us when we made enquiries with you?"

Nirala replied....

■ QUESTIONS

1. What was Nirala's reply?

2. What is the implication of this story?

■ ANSWERS

1. Nirala replied: "At that time I was not Nirala the writer, I was just one of the boys enjoying with friends."

2. Transform your personality according to the situation and circumstances. Be a child when you are at play. Children are more creative than adults. Develop humility and you will thus improve your creativity. When we mix freely with children, we imbibe their qualities. Greatness lies in simplicity and humility. Nirala was totally absorbed in play, and blissfully unaware of his Self. This is a great meditative technique. Meditation is a simple process of forgetting yourself in whatever you do.

32

Love and serve humanity at large

The world-famous pop star, Cliff Richards, was once asked to share one of the most humbling and touching experiences of his life. In answer, he reminisced about a visit he had paid to one of the Bihari refugee camps in Bangladesh. "The first morning", he said, "I must have washed my hands at least a dozen times. I didn't want to touch anything, least of all the people there. Everyone in those camps, even the babies, was covered in sores and scabs. I was bending down to one little child, mainly for the photographer's benefit and trying hard not to have too close a contact, when someone accidentally stood on the child's fingers and the child screamed out aloud with pain and I....

■ QUESTIONS

1. How did he react?

2. What is the implication of the story?

■ ANSWERS

1. The child screamed out in pain and, as a reflex, I grabbed
   hold of him, forgetting all about his dirt and sores. I
   remember now that warm little body clinging to me,
   and the crying instantly stopped. In that moment, I
   knew I had an enormous amount to learn about loving,
   but I was happy that I had at least made a start. The
   photographs of me standing ashen-faced with the little
   boy buried in my shoulder are one of my most treasured
   possessions. It hangs on the wall between my bedroom
   and bathroom, where I cannot fail to see it or remember
   it."

2. Love transcends every barrier of caste, country, creed,
   or sex. It knows no nationality, and neither does love
   judge a person depending upon his social status. We
   must all learn to express love without holding any such
   barriers. No one in this world should be looked down
   upon only because of a disease or an unavoidable filthy
   condition. Giving warmth and security and helping such
   people gives one immense satisfaction and happiness.
   Happiness is the legitimate fruit of love and service.

33
Realise the simple truth that we are slowly dying

Entering the studio early one morning, someone asked Charles Boyer how he was feeling that day. Very pleasantly, Charles Boyer answered, "Slowly dying." The person who questioned him was shocked. He went on further to add, "What's wrong with you?" Boyer replied...

■ QUESTIONS

1. What was Charles Boyer's reply?

2. What is the implication of this story?

■ ANSWERS

1. "I began to die the day I was born."

2. Death is the most certain thing in man's life, and yet it is the one that he finds most difficult to accept. We do not want to believe that we will stop existing one day. But, it is true that we begin our journey towards death the very moment we are born. The one who realizes this simple truth will never fear death.

34

Express your beauty in Love and Affection

A little girl was once studying about Abraham Lincoln – the President of the United States. She wondered how he must look as a person, and asked her father. Her father said, "My dear, I'm afraid President Lincoln is not very good-looking." The little girl carried the same image with her all through, but she was all the same extremely impressed with whatever was written about him in the newspapers. One day, after a lot of insistence, her father took her to see the President at the White House. Lincoln took her on his knee and chatted with her for a while in his usual gentle and humorous way. Suddenly, the girl shouted at her father and told him something.

■ QUESTIONS

1. What did the girl tell her father?

2. What is the implication of this story?

■ ANSWERS

1. The girl called out to her father, "Father, he is the most handsome man I've ever seen."

2. A person's deeds and his nature break all barriers between two people.

A sterling character rises above outer appearances. We must all learn to value this in a person. A person looks handsome not because of his looks, but because of what good deeds he does. Handsome is what handsome does.

35
Learn the Technique of Motivation

A foreman, who was given the charge of a gang of extremely lazy labourers, asked them to dig ten feet holes near a large steel mill. The lazy workers were further agitated when they were told to dig the holes here and there. As time went by, they kept digging, and finally they dug up nine holes. They could not understand why they were being made to dig so many holes near the factory. They also grew desperate, tired, and extremely agitated. They decided to stop right there and not to work any more. As they were about to retire, the foreman told them something which made them spring back to action forgetting all their agitation and tiredness.

■ QUESTIONS

1. What did the foreman tell them?

2. What is the implication of this story?

◼ ANSWERS

1. The foreman told them that he was actually looking for a broken pipe which supplied water to the quarters where these workmen resided. The labourers sprang back to work at once.

2. To work without a definite goal is not just uninspiring, but also difficult. On the other hand, when a man knows the purpose of what he is doing, he is able to focus better, be more sincere and diligent in what he is doing. In the absence of any specific objective, it is very difficult to get into action with full dedication and devotion. Another perspective to this is that if a person believes that he stands to gain from a particular activity, his enthusiasm rises automatically.

36
How to strengthen a Relationship

A psychology professor was well-known for his expertise, in-depth knowledge, and practical wisdom. Once, there arose a mighty quarrel among some of his students. They all fought bitterly, and for a long time there was a lot of animosity and hatred in the air. The other students were quite concerned about restoring the peace and serenity of the college atmosphere. Some approached the psychology professor for a solution. It was believed that he had a technique that was guaranteed to bring love and harmony among the students. They requested the kind professor to help them find a solution to this hatred and distrust. The professor suggested the following solution.

■ QUESTIONS

1. What was the solution given by the professor?

2. What is the implication of this story?

■ ANSWERS

1. The professor revealed the technique, "Whenever you are with anyone or you think of anyone, simply say unto yourself, 'I'm dying and this person too is dying.' Try to experience mentally the truth of these words. If every one of you agrees to practise this, there will be no bitterness any longer, and pure harmony will arise."

2. No one believes deep down that he is going to die one day. However, everyone 'knows' that he has to die one day or another, but no one 'feels or believes' that he is going to die. All the problems of the world arise out of this simple truth that no one believes in his death. A person who is reminded of his death frequently would never develop hatred and animosity towards other persons. The thought that "I am going to die and the other person is also going to die," would transform anyone to be a better person. Only then will true love prevail.

37
Overcome colour prejudice through excellence

There was once a little black boy who had witnessed the many atrocities of apartheid (racial discrimination). His family, relatives, and friends had been tortured and harassed all because of their colour. He happened to go to a country fair, and stood near a balloon man with lots of differently-coloured balloons. The balloon man allowed a red balloon to break loose and soar up high in the sky, thereby attracting children rushing in to buy some. Next, he released a blue balloon, then a yellow one, and a white one. They all went soaring up in the sky until they all disappeared. The little black boy stood looking at the black balloon for a long time, and then asked, "Sir, will the black balloon also be able to fly as high as the other ones?"

■ QUESTIONS

1. What did the balloon man reply?

2. What is the implication of this story?

ANSWERS

1. "Yes, surely my dear. It is not the colour, but what is inside the balloons that makes them fly high."

2. On the superficial level of social inter action, the colour of the skin may make a difference. Racial discrimination is one of the worst social evils of all times, since it insults the very basis of humanity. Man is equal in birth and death, and must always be treated as one, irrespective of caste, colour or creed. Racial differences cannot infiltrate where excellence prevails.

38

Nothing is Wasted Effort

Thomas Edison was once conducting research on a substitute to lead in storage batteries. He worked extensively in this pursuit, and performed close to 10,000 experiments. But, unfortunately nothing worked. One day, a friend asked him if he ever felt discouraged by this wasted effort. Edison's answer gave a new dimension to this person's life.

■ QUESTIONS

1. What did Edison reply?

2. What is the implication of this story?

■ ANSWERS

1. Edison replied, "Wasted efforts? These experiments are no waste at all. At-least I discovered 10,000 things won't work as a substitute to lead in storage batteries!"

2. No work is small or big, whatever its end results are. We should learn to see every bit of work in a positive

light, despite its result. Edison made no compromises in his efforts, but still was undeterred by his failures. When you learn to change your perspective towards small failures, you are well on your way to sure success at some point or another. Success does not come suddenly or without any setback. It takes time, hard work, and perseverance to do big things.

39

How do you avoid Criticism?

A famous musician was once very discouraged by the frequent criticism of his performance. Having been a veteran, this criticism affected him tremendously, and he seemed to be losing all his confidence. He went to his spiritual Master for some pep talk and advice. The Master said, "The critics play a very important role in one's life. They tell you what your friends will never. Don't give it too much of importance, but do think about how it can better your performance in some way or the other. If it can contribute to your growth, they're actually doing you a favour, aren't they?"

The Master said something else to the musician.

■ QUESTIONS

1. What did the Master say to convince the musician?

2. What is the implication of the story?

■ ANSWERS

1. Said the Master: "No statue was ever erected to honour a critic. Statues are for the criticized."

2. The best way to avoid criticism is to do nothing, say nothing, and be nothing. Criticism is hurled only on those who contribute something useful to society. Only the doers are criticized, and not the non-performers. The more the criticism, the greater could be the contribution. Therefore, one should not get discouraged with criticism. Moreover, learn to look constructively, so that it can only contribute to your progress.

40
Respect the Law

It was 1923. Gandhiji was serving his sentence in the Yervada jail. In those days, visitors were allowed to see the inmates only at an appointed time in the evening. One day, Kasturba came to meet Gandhiji. According to the rules of the jail, the inmates were allowed to speak to their dear ones only in the presence of the warden. But, since Gandhiji was a well-known leader, the warden did not wait there.

When it was time to leave, the warden came in to inform them. He was shocked to see both, Kasturba and Gandhiji standing still like statues, without having uttered a single word during all that time.

"Why are you two so silent? Is there a problem?" inquired the warden.

Gandhiji replied...

■ QUESTIONS

1. What was Gandhiji reply?

2. What is the implication of this story?

■ ANSWERS

1. Gandhiji replied, "I am aware of the rules of this jail. I am no different from my fellow inmates. Then, why should I be given the privilege of talking to my wife in private when the others can't? I'm sure my wife agrees with my opinion because she believes in equality too. Since you went away, we did not speak to each other because we would have then violated the rules of the jail."

2. Gandhiji is called 'Mahatma (the great soul) because of such qualities. He did not take advantage of his popularity. He obeyed the law as a common man, and as a law-abiding citizen. That was his greatness.

41
Encourage Your Child

A ten-year-old boy aspired to become a singer some day. One day, he went for a voice-audition, but was rejected outright and was told that his voice seemed like a wind hitting the window shutters. His mother, though a poor peasant woman, was well aware of her son's innate talent and encouraged the boy to continue working towards his goal. It was only because of her constant encouragement and confidence that this little boy went on to win the world with his melodious voice. He was none other than the greatest singer of all times – Enrico Caruso.

■ QUESTIONS

What is the implication of this story?

■ ANSWERS

Parents play a great role in the development of children. Every word uttered by the parents makes an indelible impression on their mind. In this context the following poem is worth quoting.

"If a child lives with criticism, he learns to condemn.

If a child lives with hostility, he learns to fight.

If a child lives with ridicule, he learns to be shy.

If a child lives with shame, he learns to feel guilty.

If a child lives with tolerance, he learns to be patient.

If a child lives with encouragement, he learns confidence.

If a child lives with praise, he learns to appreciate.

If a child lives with fairness, he learns justice.

If a child lives with security, he learns to have faith.

If a child lives with approval, he learns to like himself.

If a child lives with acceptance and friendship, he learns to find love in this world."

—Dorothy Law Holte

42
Develop the Spirit of true humility

A renowned surgeon was once seen praying before he went into the operation theatre to perform a surgery. The nurse assisting him was surprised, "Doctor, I thought that a surgeon should rely only on his own ability." The surgeon replied:

■ QUESTIONS

1. What was the surgeon's reply?

2. What is the implication of this story?

■ ANSWERS

1. The surgeon replied: "A surgeon is only human. He cannot work miracles by himself. I am certain that science couldn't have made such progress, if it weren't for something stronger than merely man's intelligence and skill. I feel so close to God when I pray before every operation, that I feel his hand guiding mine

throughout every surgery."

2. Dr. Alexis Carrel unfolds the immense strength of prayer in his book, 'Man, the Unknown'. He says, "Prayer is the most powerful form of energy one can generate. It is a force as real as terrestrial gravity. As a physician, I have seen patients rise from sure death by the sheer strength of prayer. They have recovered from chronic diseases by the serene effort of prayer. Prayer, like radium, is a source of luminous, self-generating energy by addressing themselves to the infinite source of all energy. When we pray, we link ourselves with the inexhaustible power present in the Universe."

43

Go One Step Further

❧✦❧

A sweeper working in a cinema theatre was very punctual, regular, and committed to his duties. He would not just perform these duties, but would also look after the security of the theatre.

Very often, he would be asked by the manager and the assistant manager to take over their duties, and they would often take leave from work. This sweeper conducted their duties equally well, and never once cribbed about the additional work he had to do. Once, the owner of the theatre came in for a surprise check and enquired about the upkeep of the theatre when the manager and the assistant manager were not around. The sweeper replied...

■ QUESTIONS

1. What was the sweeper's reply?

2. What is the implication of this story?

■ ANSWERS

1. "I do, Sir", the sweeper replied. Hearing his answer, the
    sweeper was instantly made the new manger of the
    theatre.

2. The world needs go-getters – people who produce
    results. When you produce results you get accepted by
    society, irrespective of your caste, creed, colour and
    even your qualifications. The world is looking for the
    man of devotion and commitment. Be committed to
    what you are expected to do, and go one step forward
    to do some extra work to become more successful in
    your life.

44
Show concern for each other

Two brothers, one bachelor and the other married, owned a farm whose fertile soil yielded abundant grain. The two brothers always made two equal parts before taking it home. Half of the grain went to one brother and the other half to another. All went well in the beginning. Then, occassionaly the married man began to think, "This is not fair. My brother is not married and he gets half the produce of the farm. Here I am, with a wife and three children. I have all the security I need for my old age. But, who will care for my poor brother when he gets old? He needs to save much more for the future than he does at present, so his need is obviously greater than mine."

With that thought, he would get out of bed, steal over to his brother's place and keep a sack full of grain into his brother's granary.

The bachelor too woke up from his sleep, and began to think, "This simply is not fair. My brother has a wife and three kids, and I'm sure the amount of produce he gets may not be enough for him. I do not have any dependents like my dear brother. And how much grain does a bachelor really need? My brother's need is obviously more than mine. He would promptly get out of bed and keep a sack full of grain into his brother's granary.

It so happened that one day, when they were rushing to each other's granary to keep the sack of grains, they banged into each other and died instantly.

Many years later, after their death, the story leaked out. The townsfolk wanted to build a temple at the very place where the two brothers had met their death.

■ QUESTIONS

1. Which place did they choose for building the temple?

2. What is the implication of this story?

■ ANSWERS

1. They chose the spot where the two brothers had met their death, for they could not think of any other place in their town that was holier than that one.

2. Exalted love expresses itself in terms of sacrifice. Love is nothing but selflessness.

45

Derive happiness through self-sacrifice

Robert Lee, the great leader of the confederate army, was once traveling along with some of his soldiers and officers by train. When the train halted at a particular station, a poor woman entered their compartment. As there was no empty seat and no one cared to offer her any, she had to stand all along, till Robert Lee spotted her and offered her his seat. At once, everyone in the compartment stood up and offered their seat to him. Lee then said something that put all of them to shame.

■ QUESTIONS

1. What did he say to all his officers and soldiers?

2. What is the implication of this story?

■ ANSWERS

1. He said, "No, gentlemen, if you can't give your seat to a poor woman, I too will not accept one from you."

2. The humility and generosity of Robert Lee is quite laudable. Enduring happiness comes out of self-denial and sacrifice of one's own comfort for the sake of others. Doing a good deed should not depend on the person's social status.

46

Practise, practise, practise...

Holman Hunt, the famous painter who painted 'The Light of the World', was once asked by a painter-admirer the technique of drawing free hand circles as perfect as his. The secret technique that Hunt told the artist, revealed the basic key to success. He said...

■ QUESTIONS

1. What secret did Holman Hunt reveal?

2. What is the implication of this story?

■ ANSWERS

1. He said, "It is very simple. All you need to do is to practise eight hours a day for forty years."

2. Practise makes perfect. Though it may sound clichéd, this is one sure-shot mantra for success in any field. Keep practising.

47

Prayer brings you closer to God

Once upon a time, in the vast kingdom of Emperor Akbar, there lived a poor but happy peasant couple, who loved each other immensely. One day, bad luck struck them, and the husband fell terribly sick. All doctors gave up on his recovery, and told his wife to prepare herself for the worst. As there was nothing else anyone could do to save her husband, the woman, with hope in her heart and strength in her soul, decided to knock at Allah's doors. She headed straight for the mosque to kneel down before the Creator himself. Covering her head with a torn veil, head bent, she walked inside the mosque with a picture of her husband's smile on her mind and Allah's presence in sight. She was numb with emotion, she could neither see nor feel anything else. As she was walking towards the mosque, she tripped and stumbled over His Highness, the Emperor Akbar himself, who was sitting there to perform *namaz*. Shocked and angry, he yelled at her, with hand half-raised as if to hit her. The woman, composed and calm, looked at him and said fearlessly.

■ QUESTIONS

1. What did she say to the Emperor?

2. What is the implication of this story?

■ ANSWERS

1. The woman said: "Your Majesty, I was so absorbed in the thought of my husband that I did not even see you here, not even when I stumbled over you. You should have been in the same trance while offering namaz to Allah because he is the most precious one in the world. And how is it that you noticed me?"

2. The Emperor was shamed into silence and later confided to his friends that a peasant woman, who was neither a scholar nor a *mulla*, had taught him the true meaning of prayer. Prayer does not consist in reciting a few lines in praise of the Almighty, but it means being one with God with total dedication and commitment.

48

Focus on whatever you do

Two women friends were driving on a highway. While one of them was driving, the other sat by her side, talking to her non-stop. She chatted, joked, and even asked a few questions. The woman driving the car did not answer any of her questions and maintained perfect silence. The talkative woman tried her best to make the other speak, but in vain. Finally, at the end of the drive, she remarked, "You have been strangely silent all through the journey. You must have something really important on your mind. Could you tell me what it is?"

■ QUESTIONS

1. What was the reply of the woman driving the car?

2. What is the implication of this story?

■ ANSWERS

1. She said: "Yes, your life and mine."

2. This story reveals the need for concentration. We must

learn to pay undivided attention to things, especially those that involve life. Sometimes people laugh, chat and joke while driving. This endangers the lives of so many persons — those in the car and those outside. Concentrated attention sharpens the intellect. The force of a person's intelligence is equal to the force of his concentration. Pay total attention to whatever you do. It is of no use if an intelligent mind keeps drifting, while nothing is impossible for the concentrated mind.

49

Honesty is the best policy

The Central National Bank of Yorkers, New York was famous for its prompt service and excellent vision. It had a massive customer following, and the bank dealt with the customers with trust and honesty. The bank wanted to prove that the general public too can be trusted for their honesty. To prove this the bank placed a big bowl of small change for the people to take by putting currency notes of equal value. There was no supervision and the scheme had to work on the total honesty of the people. At the end of the very first day of its experiment the bank found......

■ QUESTIONS

1. What did the bank find at the end of the first day?

2. What is the implication of this story?

■ ANSWERS

1. The bank found the book balanced exactly to every penny.

2. By and large, people are honest and trustworthy. Only a miniscule segment of people turn to be dishonest and criminal. It is better to trust people than to mistrust.

50
Develop large-heartedness

Rabbi Shemelke was a kind-hearted man, who cared a lot for everyone regardless of his caste, creed, and profession. One day, as he sat in his garden, a beggar came to his doorstep. Unfortunately, the rabbi had no money to give him. He ransacked his wife's drawer, took a ring from it, and gave it to him. When on her return, she found her ring was missing, the wife raised a hue and cry. Learning from her husband what he had done, she asked him to run after the beggar, since the ring was worth fifty *dinars*.

The rabbi ran after the beggar in hot pursuit, and ultimately caught him.

■ QUESTIONS

1. What did the rabbi tell the beggar?

2. What is the implication of this story?

■ ANSWERS

1. The rabbi told him, "I have just learned that the ring is fifty *dinars*. See that no one cheats you by giving you anything lesser than that."

2. The world continues to survive thanks to some kind-hearted and generous people like the rabbi in this story.

51

What is true Prayer?

A wise man would give regular lectures to his disciples. He was a very learned man, and always shared something good and positive with them. One day, he was talking to them about his prayer habits during his days as a youngster, "I was a revolutionary then, and all my prayers were requests to the Lord to change the world. As I approached the middle age, my prayers became requests to change the family and friends. But, now that I am an old man, I have a different prayer altogether."

■ QUESTIONS

1. When the wise man became old, what did his prayer become?

2. What is the implication of this story?

■ ANSWERS

1. When the wise man became old, his prayer was a request to the Lord to bestow on him the grace to change his own Self.

2. It is futile to want to change the whole world. Prayer is
    a form of auto-suggestion that works wonders on
    oneself, not on others. It is the most powerful form of
    energy that one can generate. As Alexis Carrel put its,
    "The influence of prayer on the human mind and body
    is as demonstrable as that of secreting glands. Its results
    can be measured in terms of increased physical buoyancy,
    greater intellectual vigour, moral stamina and a deeper
    understanding of the realities underlying human
    relationships. True prayer is a way of life: the truest
    life is literally a way of prayer."

52

Reduce stress and tension

The managing director of one of the largest commercial interests in the world was sitting in his New York office, talking to a client one morning. Suddenly, his secretary came into the room looking harassed, a sheaf of impressive documents in her hands. She talked excitedly and at great length seeking to impress upon his chief the desperate nature of the problem. "Mrs. Jones," said the managing director. "Please read rule three again."

The secretary looked startled. She looked at the papers and smiled, before leaving the room. Overcome by curiosity, the client asked the managing director to explain rule three.

■ QUESTIONS

1. What was the rule three?

2. What are rules one and two?

3. What is the implication of this story?

■ ANSWERS

1. The rule three was about not taking oneself too seriously.

2. There were no other rules in the company, only rule three.

3. This story emphasizes that nothing should be taken too seriously. When things are taken too seriously, people automatically suffer from stress and tension. And when a person suffers from stress and tension, one tends to have lower productivity. If one wants to improve one's efficiency, one must be stress-free and tension-free.

53
Trust people and they will be trustworthy

A boy had become notorious in the class for his habit of stealing. The teacher wanted to improve his ways by talking it out with him. But, he simply would not change. Although she did not believe in punishment, she knew she had to do something about this, before it got worse.

She once called him, gave him some money to go and purchase some things for the class. When the boy returned with the things and the change, the teacher took it without even counting it. She spoke to the class appreciating the boy's honesty and his trustworthiness. He was shocked to hear this, since he had indeed stolen some money from what she had given him. He realized his mistake and never again stole a penny.

■ QUESTIONS

What is the implication of this story?

■ ANSWERS

The teacher showed the boy that she really trusted him, and this incident made him a new person. Trust can work wonders in reforming people.

54
Who is an enlightened person?

A village girl once became an unwed mother. The villagers were shocked and punished her with several beatings, forcing her to reveal the name of her baby's father. To everyone's shock, she told the world that it was none other than the Zen Master who lived on the outskirts of the village. The villagers went to his monastery, rudely disturbed his meditation, and denounced him as a hypocrite. "You have sinned against a girl from our village. You will have to take care of the mother and the baby." All that the Master said was, "Is it so?"

He took the baby in his arms, and looked after it very well with lots of love and affection. But his name was tainted forever. All his disciples abandoned him, one after the other. This went on for a year at the end of which, the girl could not bear it any longer.

She went back to the villagers and confessed that she had lied to them. The father of the baby was not the Zen Master, but her next door neighbour. The villagers went to the Master and informed him what has happened. He replied...

■ QUESTIONS

1. What was the reaction of the Master?

2. What is the implication of this story?

■ ANSWERS

1. All that the Master said was, "Is it so?

2. When he was accused the only statement he made was "Is it so?" A person who takes praise and blame with equanimity is the truly enlightened one. Although it takes immense mental strength, one must always try to achieve such a bent of mind.

55

Achieve great things through hard work

ord Louis Mountbatten, the last Viceroy of India, was known all over the world for his amazing ability and brilliance in dealing with the most complex problems. Once, he was at a press conference, fielding several questions with great skill. One of the journalists praised him, and asked him the secret to all his achievements. To this, Lord Mountbatten gave an answer that got him a standing ovation from everyone present.

■ QUESTIONS

1. What was his answer?

2. What is the implication of this story?

■ ANSWERS

1. Lord Mountbatten said, "The truth is that I am a very ordinary person, and if I have any success, it is only due to hard work and sincerity."

2. Success can be achieved only through hard work and dedication. If you keep working towards your goal, there is nothing that cannot be achieved by you. In the garland of success hard work is the thread.

56
Never give up

❧❧❧

Mishaps do leave a scar on our heart, but they always have a way of teaching something very relevant to us. In 1914, Edison's factories were completely destroyed by fire, thus causing a loss of more than two million dollars worth of equipment. When the factory was being consumed by the angry flames, Edison's son was looking out desperately for his father. He saw his father standing near the fire, the son's heart ached for his aged father. Edison saw his son and said, "Where's your mother? Call her to see this spectacle. She's never going to see anything like this in her entire life again." His wife came and saw the catastrophe. The next morning, both went for a walk. Walking through the remains of his majestic factories, the 67-year-old Edison said something to his wife that brought back her lost smile and lit up her dull face.

■ QUESTIONS

1. What did Edison say to his wife?

2. What is the implication of this story?

■ ANSWERS

1. Edison said, "There is a great value in disaster. All our mistakes are burned up. Thank God, we can start afresh."

2. To never give up is the lesson that we learn from this story. Looking at defeat in a positive light is the key to bounce back to success. Edison's name will forever be written in golden words in the world of scientific research.

57
The efficacy of stories and parables

A Master delivered his preachings through parables and stories, and his disciples loved it. They always listened to his teachings with rapt attention and great pleasure. But, there was also some occasional frustration as the disciples longed for something deeper. Despite all their complaints, the Master remained unmoved and had only one answer to their objections.

■ QUESTIONS

1. What was the Master's answer?

2. What is the implication of this story?

■ ANSWERS

1. The Master said, "You have yet to understand, my dear disciples, that the shortest distance between a human being and the truth is a story."

2. Stories convey the truth in a graphic manner. Although we often relate stories with children, we must not underestimate its power to drive home a deep truth.

58

Do more than you are paid for

The Managing Director of a company had a secretary working for him for quite sometime. One day, he decided to give her a raise for all the hard work she had put in for many years. Wanting to surprise her with the good news, he scribbled his decision on a piece of paper, went to her chamber and asked her to type out the note. The lady simply glanced at the paper, and continued with her work. In fact, she did not even complete her typing work, and left the note as it was. As for the boss' note, she had not even noticed it.

■ QUESTIONS

1. What was the reaction of the boss?

2. What is the implication of this story?

■ ANSWERS

1. The boss changed his decision to promote his secretary immediately. An employee is promoted in order to

motivate him, and thereby improve his productivity. However, disregard for the kind gesture surely makes the person regret the decision to do so. Because of her negligence, the secretary lost her chance of promotion.

2. Every employer wants to employ those who are prepared to work a little extra than what they are supposed to do. True dedication and commitment always pays in the long run.

59

God helps those who help themselves

Apoor woman was abandoned by her husband. Upon hearing this, her neighbour rushed to wipe her tears and console her. To her surprise, instead of finding a distraught, helpless woman, she found a happy, cheerful and confident woman. "You look very happy and unaffected. Aren't you worried about your future? How are you going to support yourself? Have you any means of support whatsoever?" The other woman's answer was a lesson in itself.

■ QUESTIONS

1. What was the answer of the abandoned woman?

2. What is the implication of this story?

■ ANSWERS

1. The woman replied, "I have three major support factors in life: my hands, my good health and my God. I don't

need the support of anybody else."

2. The story of this woman reminds me of the following
poem:

"Depend not on another, rather

Upon thyself, Trust to thine own exertions

Subjection to another's will, only gives pain

True happiness consists in self-reliance."

60
Learn to forgive

❦

Aschool boy was once sent to the Principal for
having committed a serious mistake. After hearing
all the facts, the Principal took out a blank book,
and wrote the boy's name. Proceeding to write down the
complaint, he said to the boy.....

■ QUESTIONS

1. What did the Principal say?

2. What is the implication of this story?

■ ANSWERS

1. The Principal made a note in pencil in the note book,
   and said to the boy: "I am making this memorandum
   in pencil and I will not take your mistake very seriously.
   In fact, if you are not sent to me again this year, I shall
   erase this from my book and no one will ever know
   anything about it."

2. Mercy is a great virtue that every person must learn to
   inculcate.

61

Be content with what you have

Quaker once put up a sign on his vacant piece of land, "Land available for the one who is truly satisfied in life."

A wealthy farmer residing close by stopped to read the sign and thought, "Since my dear friend the Quaker is so willing to part with the land, let me claim it before anyone else does. I'm a rich man. I've got everything I'll ever need, so I definitely qualify."

With that he went to the Quaker and explained what he was there for. "And are you satisfied in life?," the Quaker asked.

"Sure I am, for I have everything I need."

The Quaker responded to his request.

■ QUESTIONS

1. What was the Quaker's response?

2. What is the implication of this story?

■ ANSWERS

1. "Friend", said the Quaker, "if you're so satisfied in life, why do you want the land?"

2. While others strive for wealth, the enlightened ones are satisfied with whatever they possess. Being contented with just a little bit is to be as rich as kings.

62

Accept the uniqueness of an individual

Two men walking down a street in London passed a cathedral. There was music being played in the cathedral. One man commented. "Listen to the music. Isn't it wonderful?" The other man replied:

■ QUESTIONS

1. What was the other man's reply?

2. What is the implication of this story?

■ ANSWERS

1. The other man replied, "What music? I cannot hear any music. There is so much noise coming from the cathedral. It is blocking all the music."

2. As they say, one man's food is another man's poison. People like different things, they have different choices. Every person in this world has a right to choose and decide his preferences.

63
Guesswork doesn't work

A priest was very fond of children and dogs. He would regularly feed all the dogs in his neighbourhood. Being extremely popular among the kids, he got along very well with all of them. It was his birthday, and so, all the children came excitedly with birthday greetings and gifts to wish him. The Father took the gift-wrapped parcel from little Mary, and said, "Ah! I see you have brought me a book." (Mary's father ran a bookstore in town.)

"Yes, how did you know?"

"Father always knows!", the Father proudly exclaimed.

"And you, Tommy, have brought me a sweater," said the Father picking up the parcel that Tommy held out to him. (Tommy's father was a dealer in woolen goods). "That's right, Father. How did you know?"

"Father always knows!" the Father once again replied.

And so, it went on till Bobby's box. The wrapping paper was wet. (Bobby's father sold wines and liquors.)

So Father said, "Hmm, I see you have brought me a bottle
of wine or perhaps some liquor, and spilled some of it."

"Wrong, Father!"

The Father's fingers were all wet and he put one of the
fingers in his mouth, but he could not find the answer.

■ QUESTIONS

1. What was Bobby's gift to the Father?

2. What is the implication of this story?

■ ANSWERS

1. Bobby had gifted the Father a puppy.

2. Nobody can claim to be omniscient.

64
Money has power

A man once placed a bet with his friend about the power of money. He argued that money could buy anything. To prove it, he even went up to the priest of the big church and said, "Father, my dog died yesterday. I would like to offer a mass in his memory?"

The Father was naturally outraged at this request. "We don't offer masses for animals here. You might try the new denomination down the road. They'll probably pray for your dead dog."

The man did not lose hope and persisted. Much to his friend's surprise, the Father agreed and the friend lost the bet.

■ QUESTIONS

1. What do you think the man told the Father?

2. What is the implication of this story?

■ ANSWERS

1. The man told the Father, "I really loved the dog, and I would love him to have a decent send-off. I don't know what it is customary to offer on such occasions, but do you think five hundred thousand dollars will do?"

2. The power of money can overpower even the mind of a saint. In the ultimate analysis, everyone is striving to get as much money as possible. It can nearly buy almost anything we want.

65

Be courteous – you may reap a friendship

Aman engaged a taxi for the day. After having traveled around the city, when he took out his wallet to pay, the taxi driver refused to take any money from him.

■ QUESTIONS

1. Why did the taxi driver refuse payment?

2. What is the implication of this story?

■ ANSWERS

1. The taxi driver said: "I have been driving the taxi for 20 years. In all these twenty years, you're the first person who has been so polite and courteous to me. I cannot take money from the friend that I have found in you.

2. He who sows courtesy reaps friendship: he who plants kindness gathers love; he who has won the friendship of a friend has won it all.

66

Develop the virtue of forgiveness

Once, the son of King Louis XVI was taken prisoner by a rival nation, and sent to the torture room. The French Dauphin was held prisoner by one of the most difficult jailors. The jailor had been waiting to lay his hands upon this poor helpless child, for having been born into the royal family. Everyday, the jailor would increase his torture a little more, and each time, the child would quietly bear it all, praying to God.

One day, the jailor asked him, "What would you do, Capeto, if the Vendeanos set you free? What would you do with me? Would you have me hanged?"

■ QUESTIONS

1. What was the answer of the little boy?

2. What is the implication of this story?

■ ANSWERS

1. The little boy smiled and said: "I would forgive you."

2. Forgiveness is one of the noblest virtues of man. As St. Francis of Sales once said, "If, someone in hatred were to pluck out my left eye, I think I could look kindly at him with my right eye. If he plucked that one out too, I would still have the heart with which to love him."

67

Enjoy the realistic present

This is the story of a very renowned rabbi, Mokshe. He was well-known for his wisdom and warmth. He died in an accident, leaving many of his disciples depressed and disheartened. Another rabbi named Mendel once visited his monastery, and was stunned at the overwhelming love for the deceased rabbi amongst all his disciples. He asked one of his disciples there, "What did your teacher give importance to?"

The disciple gave it a moment's reflection, and gave an answer that made the rabbi realize how great rabbi Mokshe was.

■ QUESTIONS

1. What was the disciple's answer?

2. What is the implication of this story?

■ ANSWERS

1. The disciple answered, "Rabbi Mokshe gave a lot of

importance to whatever he happened to be doing at the moment."

2. Holiness consists in living in the present. Being aware of the present moment brings enlightenment. The man who lives in the present, forgetful of the past and indifferent to the future, is the man of wisdom. The best preparation for tomorrow's work is to do your work today itself. The best preparation for life to come is done by living in the here and now. Live right up to your highest and your best. Learn to seal the dead past, not to worry about the unborn future, but live and enjoy the realistic present.

68
Don't Compare

A beautiful little sparrow lived atop a huge banyan tree. She would look at all the other birds flying in the sky, and felt very small in comparison. She hated the way she looked, "You gave the peacock such beautiful colours, you gave a melodious voice to the nightingale, but me, you did not give me anything. Why?" To this God replied...

■ QUESTIONS

1. What was God's reply?

2. What is the implication of this story?

■ ANSWERS

1. God said – "You were not made to suffer, and now you are making the same foolish mistake that human beings usually do. Just be yourself and you will be the best. Understand your uniqueness and enjoy being just the way you were meant to be."

2. Everyone is created in the image of God. He has made
    each and every creation a unique one. We must learn to
    see this fact as a positive life force, not something that
    makes one inferior or superior to another. Most people
    mar their lives with feelings of inferiority, and thus put
    obstacles between themselves and happiness.

69

Derive joy in giving

William Allen White, the famous sage of Emporia, USA presented his native city with a 50-acre wooded plot as a site for a park. While doing so, Mr. White declared, "This is the last kick in a fistful of dollars I am getting rid of. I have tried to teach people that there are three kicks in every dollar that give the most wonderful feeling of all."

■ QUESTIONS

1. What are those three kicks in each dollar?

2. What is the implication of this story?

■ ANSWERS

1. He said: 'The three kicks are — one when you earn it, the other when you have it, and the third when you give it away."

2. Fools earn and hoard their money. It is natural to earn and enjoy the fruits of one's own labour. However,

great men are those that earn and then spend the money
for the upliftment of society and humanity as a whole.
There is great joy in giving, that only the wise can
realize.

70
Experience the joy of giving

❧

Henry Ford, the father of car manufacturing, was once holidaying in Dublin. A delegation from an orphanage came to his hotel asking for some contribution for a new building. Mr. Ford immediately wrote out a cheque for 2,000 pounds for this noble cause. The next morning, a Dublin newspaper carried a front-page headline that Ford gave 20,000 pounds as contribution for the Irish orphanage. That morning, the director of the orphanage came rushing to Ford's suite to apologize and offered to phone the editor of the paper with a correction.

"Never mind", Ford said as he wrote another cheque of 18,000 pounds. "You can have this cheque only on one condition."

■ QUESTIONS

1. What was the condition?

2. What is the implication of this story?

■ ANSWERS

1. Ford said: "When the new building opens, I want this inscription on it: I was a stranger and you took me in."

2. To be a big man takes a bit of everything. Ford showed a great sense of humour along with equal magnanimity. While the phrase 'take in' meant to give shelter, it also meant to be fooled, deceived or cheated.

71

When should you begin the education of your child?

Once, a young mother approached Aristotle, "When should I begin the training of my child?" Aristotle asked, "How old is your child?" She replied that her child was five years old. At that moment, Aristotle cried out...

■ QUESTIONS

1. What did Aristotle cry out?

2. What is the implication of this story?

■ ANSWERS

1. Aristotle cried out, "Hurry home, you are already five years late."

2. The education of a child begins as soon as it is born. The child's primary influences are his parents, because they are the ones who give him good values in the school called 'home'.

72

Understand the value of knowledge

Once, an important machine in a factory stopped functioning totally. As a result, all the work in the entire factory came to a standstill. All the foremen and engineers in the factory tried their best to get the machine working, but in vain. Ultimately, an expert was called in to set the machine right. After having examined the machine thoroughly, he took a hammer and struck the machine at a particular spot. That very moment, the machine started functioning smoothly.

The expert sent a bill for Rs. 10,000 for the work done. Obviously, the expert was questioned about why they should pay so much money for just taking the hammer and hitting the machine in a particular place, and that too only once. The expert modified the bill, and sent it back to the factory for payment.

■ QUESTIONS

1. What was the modification made by the expert in the bill?

2. What is the implication of this story?

■ ANSWERS

1. The modified version of the bill is as follows:

	Rs.
Charges for striking the machine with a hammer	0,005
Charges for knowing where to strike	9,995
Total	10,000

2. Knowledge is power. It takes a lot of hard work, intelligence, and effort to acquire knowledge. One pays an expert not just for his time, but also for his expertise.

73
Age is what you think in your mind

The homas Edison was among those few people who firmly believed that age is what you think in your mind, and you are only as old as you think you are. On his eightieth birthday, a close friend suggested that he should now slacken his pace and should start taking time out for himself now. "You should have a hobby of some kind. Why don't you take up golf?" said the friend. Edison replied...

■ QUESTIONS

1. What did Edison tell his friend?

2. What is the implication of this story?

■ ANSWERS

1. Edison said, "I am not old enough yet."

2. Even at the ripe age of eighty, Edison joked about

himself being very young. Age does not depend upon the number of years spent on earth. On the contrary, it depends on how you spend those years. Age is no bar for those who have a burning desire to accomplish something great in life.

74
Be Tactful

Amighty ruler in a faraway land loved to eat cabbages. He enjoyed eating them in any form, and would often ask his cook to prepare them. The poor cook would try his best to make as many varieties of the cabbage to please his master. Once, the Master got a bad stomach due to eating too much of it. He immediately changed his stand, now claiming that the cabbage was the most horrible thing on earth. This time too, the cook agreed with him. The king was annoyed at the cook's servility, and asked him how he could agree with both his statements. The cook replied:

■ QUESTIONS

1. What was the cook's reply?

2. What is the implication of this story?

■ ANSWERS

1. The cook replied: "I am your servant, Your Majesty, and not that of the cabbage."

2. Tact wins the heart.

75
Practice makes perfect

❧❧❧

Paderewski, a renowned violinist, would practise for ten to twelve hours a day, even when he was at the pinnacle of success. Once after his performance, one of his fans, who also happened to be a violinist, asked him the secret to his success. Paderewski told him…

■ QUESTIONS

1. What was the secret to Paderewski's success?

2. What is the implication of this story?

■ ANSWERS

1. He said, "I can trustfully say that if I neglect my practice for one day, I can see the difference. If I neglect it for two days, my critics discover. And if I neglect it for more than three days, the whole world knows it."

2. To become truly successful, you must constantly hone your craft, and not let success make you complacent. It doesn't take too long for a craftsman's tools to rust and be rendered useless, if they are not used regularly.

76

You are both your present and future

A man who lived a luxurious life was feeling frustrated and unhappy. Though he was an ambitious person, he did not work on his goals in a systematic manner. He kept pursuing his goals, and in the process lost track of his present. Naturally, his work suffered. As a result, he became unhappy. He tried to introspect to understand the problem in a better way, but somehow could not figure out exactly what was responsible for his messy state of affairs.

Finally, he approached an enlightened person and told him about his problem. After listening to him, the sage remarked....

■ QUESTIONS

1. What was the sage's remark?

2. What is the implication of this story?

■ ANSWERS

1. The sage remarked: "My dear man, the cause of your unhappy state of mind is none other than yourself. You are chasing a mirage when in fact, your goal is quite clear in front of you. Please understand that if your gaze is fixed on something far away, you're surely going to trip your step."

2. Most of us deceive ourselves by thinking that if we achieve our future goals we could be happy. We do not realize that we have to face our present and our future with equal attention. We should not look at the destination hoping to find our happiness there. True happiness is found along the way to your goals, during the journey and not at the end of the journey.

77
Motivation in a lighter Vein

When the recession was at its peak, industries were deteriorating. Survival had become very tough. The President of a company made an important announcement to all his employees.

■ QUESTIONS

1. What was the announcement?

2. What is the implication of this story?

■ ANSWERS

1. The announcement was:

   To all the employees: Due to increased competition and a desire to stay in business, we find it necessary to institute a new policy: We ask of you, the esteemed employees of this organization, that somewhere between the time that you walk into office and walk out of it, you could set aside some time. This, of course, would not mean infringing too much on the time usually devoted to very important activities like lunch breaks, coffee breaks, rest periods, story sessions, ticket-selling, vacation planning, important phone calls to friends and relatives, re-hashing of yesterday's TV programs, and discussions on possible outcomes of cricket matches. We request the kind co-operation of each employee to try his best to utilize this time known as the 'WORK BREAK.'

2. Many employees do not take their jobs seriously enough. The net result of their negligence leads to losses for the company. The announcement made by the President is a creative solution. The employees appreciated the light vein in which the announcement was made. They took the issue seriously, and started working hard to produce huge profits for the company.

78

How do we get enlightenment?

Aman longing to get enlightenment undertook a long journey in search of a Master. After a hazardous journey, he found a Master who was an enlightened soul. The conversation between them went on as follows:

'Where shall I look for enlightenment?'

'Right here.'

'When will it happen?'

'It is happening right now.'

'Then why don't I experience it?'

'Because you do not look.'

'What should I look for?'

'Nothing. Just look.'

'At what?'

'Anything your eyes rest on.'

'Must I look in a special way?'

'No. The ordinary way will do.'

'But don't I always look the ordinary way?'

'No.'

'Why do you say so?'

Ultimately, the Master gave his reply.

■ QUESTIONS

1. What did Master reply ultimately?

2. What is the implication of this story?

■ ANSWERS

1. "Because, in order to look, you have to be here. You're mostly somewhere else," said the Master.

2. This story brings out the phenomenon of the wavering nature of the human mind. The mind is like a mischievous monkey jumping from place to place, person to person, and ideas to ideas. If we observe the functioning of the mind, we may notice how fast it switches from one object to another. Enlightenment consists in living in the present totally and completely. Living in the present moment is enlightenment. To achieve an enlightened state of mind, one must train the mind to live in the here and now.

79
Conquer your worries

A woman who tended to worry over mundane things was once given a diamond-studded bracelet to keep. Her friend was going on a tour, and she trusted this friend to take good care of the bracelet in her absence. This woman, being worried about the safety of the bracelet, decided to buy a stronger casket in which to keep it. But the jeweller to whom she went to buy the casket simply took one look at the bracelet and commented....

■ QUESTIONS

1. What was the jeweller's comment?

2. What is the implication of this story?

■ ANSWERS

1. The jeweller informed the lady that the bracelet was not worth a new casket. He told her that all the diamonds were artificial. The lady was at first quite stunned by the news, but then she exclaimed, "Thank heavens, all my worries are now over".

2. We attach too much of importance to certain
   unnecessary issues in life, and therefore create worries
   for us. But, the solution for this problem lies in our
   own hands. It is only when we consciously decide to
   put an end to it, do we really put an end to our worries.

80
Know that you know little

One day, Thomas Alva Edison, the great scientist was invited to a school to speak to young students and to encourage them. Edison enjoyed spending time with them. He spoke to the students about his experience in the scientific field. The students too were very excited to meet such a great personality, and asked many questions. He answered each and every question very patiently. One of the students asked him, "How did you acquire so much knowledge?"

To this, Edison replied...

■ QUESTIONS

1. What was Edison's reply?

2. What is the implication of this story?

■ ANSWERS

1. Edison replied, "By telling others that I don't know, but that I was very keen to learn."

2. Wisdom and knowledge comes first from humility, and
    then by constantly seeking knowledge in any form. One
    must have almost a kind of desperation to learn
    something new. The moment you believe yourself to be
    learned or wise, you begin your journey towards Doom.
    Vanity is a sure way to finish oneself. In this context
    the words of Isaac Newton are worth quoting.

    "I do not know what I may appear to the world, but to
    myself, I seem to have been only like a boy playing on
    the seashore and diverting myself in, now and then,
    finding a smooth pebble or a prettier shell than ordinary,
    whilst the great ocean of truth lay all undiscovered
    before us." Such is the humility of great people which
    is perhaps the secret to their greatness.

81

Make every second of your life a masterpiece

Socrates was in prison, and was to be executed the next morning. Just then, he heard a fellow prisoner sing a very difficult lyric by a famous poet. On hearing this, Socrates begged the man to teach him the lyric. "Why should you learn now? Are you not going to die tomorrow morning?", asked the singer. To which, Socrates answered:

■ QUESTIONS

1. What was Socrates' answer?

2. What is the implication of this story?

■ ANSWERS

1. "So that I can die peacefully with the understanding that I have learnt one more thing in life" was the great philosopher's reply.

2. We must thank God for every moment that we spend on this beautiful earth. People like Socrates made every second of their wakeful state a masterpiece. Every second provides us an opportunity to learn and grow.

82

The predicament of having two wives

Kareem had just got married, and was leading his married life quite happily. One day, he happened to meet his friend Saleem, at a grocer's shop. Kareem started speaking to his friend about his married life, and how happy he was. Now, Saleem had two wives. He told Kareem that if he was so happy being married to one, his marital bliss would surely be doubled if he married once more.

Kareem readily agreed, and got married once more. After the second marriage, Kareem got into a major problem. Neither woman would be ready to stay with him. The first one because he had married another woman, and the second one because he already had a wife.

Dejected, Kareem went to the mosque to spend the night. There, he found Saleem sleeping comfortably on the veranda of the mosque. Kareem woke him, and asked him why he was sleeping there when he had two wives. Saleem replied:

■ QUESTIONS

1. What was Saleem's reply?

2. What is the implication of this story?

■ ANSWERS

1. Saleem said, "I felt so lonesome in this mosque, and so badly missed having some company here!"

2. Do not get carried away by another's advice. Think over the pros and cons of it, before you take any decision.

83

Convert bandage into badge of honour

Jawaharlal Nehru's aged mother, Smt. Swaruprani, was a great patriot herself, and worked a lot for the country's freedom struggle. Once, while leading a political procession, she got hit on her head by some mischief-makers. She fainted and fell down on the ground, bleeding profusely. Later on, a police officer took her in his car to Anand Bhavan where she lived. Jawaharlal was obviously very upset with the whole episode, and very worried too. One month later, Nehru was kept in the jail in Bareilley, and Swaruprani had gone to visit him with a bandage still on her head. When asked why she had taken the trouble to come there to meet him in spite of her unhealed wound, she joked about her injury and said .....

■ QUESTIONS

1. What did she say?

2. What is the implication of this story?

■ ANSWERS

1. She said, "Jawahar, this is not a mere bandage for me, but a badge of honour. I am very proud of it, and even enjoy flaunting it."

2. Any wound suffered for the country's good is a badge of honour, and a matter of immense pride. People have willingly laid down their lives for the country. They are an example that we all must follow.

84

Shun Hypocrisy

❧

A teacher once brought a box of chocolates to her class, along with a book of wisdom. She placed the two things on the table next to each other, and asked her students to choose one. All the students crowded around the book of wisdom, and commented seriously upon how interesting it would be to read the book. There was however, one who opened the box of chocolates, and began gorging on them with great pleasure. Noticing the doubtful gaze of all the other students, the teacher commented:

■ QUESTIONS

1. What was the teacher's comment?

2. What is the implication of this story?

■ ANSWERS

1. "I can see just as much wisdom in the box of chocolates as in the book of wisdom," said the teacher.

2. The student who chose the box of chocolate was someone who was true to his heart. Hypocrisy does not have a long life. We must learn to shun hypocrisy, and embrace the true calling of our heart.

85

Aim at Perfection

Thomas Gray's masterpiece poem, 'Elegy written in a country churchyard', is an immensely famous poem, so much so that it has earned its due place in the British museum. But, there are still many who do not know that, it was not until the seventy-fifth version that the poet was satisfied with his work.

■ QUESTIONS

1. What is the implication of this story?

■ ANSWERS

1. Perfection is not achieved easily. It takes undying commitment and a deep passion to achieve perfection in whatever you do. If you aim at perfection and work hard towards it, there is nothing that can keep you away from it.

86

How do you distinguish fate from destiny?

Once, there was an unhappy woman who went to the Master to complain about her destiny. The Master told her, "But it is you who makes your own destiny." The woman replied, "But, surely I am not responsible for being born as a woman?" The Master merely said...

■ QUESTIONS

1. What did the Master say?

2. What is the implication of this story?

■ ANSWERS

1. The Master said, "Your birth as a woman is your fate. That you can't change. But, what you make out of your fate is your destiny."

2. Fate is a fact of life. There is nothing superstitious

about it. Many things happen in our life without our knowledge and control. These things fall under the category of fate. Birth is fate. Similarly death too is fate. They are not under our control. But destiny is in our hands. It is shaped by the quality of our thoughts, feelings, and actions.

87
Be Optimistic

This is a tale of two buckets who regularly went to the well every morning. Said one, "This is a miserable life, no matter how full I am when I come out of the well, I always go back empty." "Dear me," said the other bucket cheerfully. "I never thought of it like that, but......

■ QUESTIONS

1. What did the other bucket reply?

2. What is the implication of this story?

■ ANSWERS

1. "It seems to me so wonderful that no matter how often I go back to the well, I always feel I am ready to quench someone's thirst once again."

2. Life gives the same chance to everyone, but it is up to each one of us how we look at it, and what we make out of it. We should cultivate an optimistic tempera-

ment, and must always see the positive side of things in everything. If we sit down and lament over the imperfection of our bodies, and minds, or the situations that we face, we will simply wallow in self-pity and will waste our life.

88

Forgive with a sincere heart

Aholy monk in an ashram had an antique Bible of rare value. Once, man came to the ashram to visit the monk. Although he came with an intention of becoming a disciple of the holy monk, he soon was tempted to steal the Bible. When the holy monk went for scripture reading, he found the Bible missing and knew at once that the visitor had taken it. But he did not send after him for fear that it might add the sin of perjury to that of the theft.

Now the person who stole the book went to an antique shop to sell the book. He wanted 100 pounds for it. The shopkeeper said, "Give me the book so that I may find out if it is worth that much money." As luck would have it, he took the book to the holy man and said, "Sir, take a look at this and please do tell me if it is worth as much as 100 pounds."

The holy man said, "Yes, it is a fine book of great value, and at 100 pounds it is a great bargain."

So the shopkeeper went back to the seller and said, "Here is your money. I showed the book to the holy man in the ashram, and he said it was worth that much money."

The man was stunned, "Was that all he said? Did he say anything else?"

"No, he did not say a word. Why do you ask?"

■ QUESTIONS

1. What was the reaction of the man who had stolen the book and wanted to sell it?

2. What is the implication of this story?

■ ANSWERS

1. The man said, "Well, I have changed my mind, and don't want to sell the book after all." He went back to the holy man, fell at his feet and begged forgiveness. He requested the holy man to take the book back. "No, brother, keep it. It is my gift to you." But the man said, "If you don't take it back, I shall have no peace." After that, the person joined the ashram, and served the holy man for the rest of his life.

2. Forgiveness reforms the most hardened of criminals. It has a far more positive influence and works very well at correcting a flaw. "There are many kinds of alms, the giving of which helps us to obtain pardon for our sins; but none is greater than that, by which we forgive from our heart a sin, that some one has committed against us."

— St. Augustine of Hippo

89

The higher the cost, greater is the value

Once there was a couple who had a beautiful Dalmatian for a pet. After a few years, this dog became pregnant, and soon delivered five little puppies. Now, the couple was in a dilemma about how to dispose off the five attractive puppies they had just recently acquired. The man spoke to many people to take them as a gift but no one was interested. They even announced it over the local radio, but unfortunately, there were no buyers. Finally, when a neighbour visited them, he was told about the problem. He advised them how to dispose of their puppies.

■ QUESTIONS

1. What was the advice given by the neighbour?

2. What is the implication of this story?

■ ANSWERS

1. The neighbour advised the couple to advertise that the puppies were being sold at twenty-five dollars each.

2. Anything given free of cost has no value. The higher the cost, the greater is their value.

90
Set an example

During the American revolutionary war, preparations for a battle were going on. At one of these places, a man in civilian dress noticed a Corporal address his men arrogantly to lift a heavy beam. The man went up to the Corporal, and asked him why he himself did not join the men in lifting the load. The Corporal retorted, "But I am a Corporal." At that point, the man in civilian dress helped the soldiers in the task. He then went up to the Corporal, and told him something that left him absolutely speechless.

■ QUESTIONS

1. What did the man tell the corporal?

2. What is the implication of this story?

■ ANSWERS

1. "Mr. Corporal, whenever you don' have enough men to do a job, call on your Commander-in-Chief and I shall

be glad to offer all the help." With that, George
Washington put on his coat and left the place.

2. Dignity reflects in the person who addresses every person
   with respect. No work is too big or too small for any
   man to do. Work should be done by everyone, without
   being ashamed of doing it.

91
Be Tactful

Henry Ward Beecher was a noted preacher. There were many people who loved him, but there were also those who condemned him. Beecher was especially known for his quick wit that reflected in his teachings. No one could fool the great preacher so easily. Ward Beecher would often conduct mass gatherings, and try his best to put people on the right path. At these gatherings, he would ask people to write down their problems on a piece of paper and drop it in a box nearby. He would then read out these one by one aloud and offer solutions. One day, he received an envelope carrying inside a sheet of paper with just one word written in the centre. "FOOL." Ward Beecher then made a public announcement to which the entire gathering roared in laughter...

■ QUESTIONS

1. What did Beecher announce?

2. What is the implication of this story?

■ ANSWERS

1. He announced that till date he had received many letters in which the writers had forgotten to sign their names. But this was the first instance in which the writer had only signed his name and forgotten to write the letter.

2. This was his way of politely rebuking the anonymous writer.

92

Accept a mistake gracefully

D r. Samuel Johnson brought out a dictionary which was very well-received by the public as well as by the critics. To celebrate the success of this publication, a grand dinner party was arranged in honour of Dr. Johnson. During the party, everybody appreciated the quality and contents of the dictionary. Dr. Johnson too charmed everyone present there with his intellectual talk about his latest work. While everybody was praising the dictionary, an old lady interrupted them, and expressed her astonishment that there was indeed an error in the great scholar's work and pin-pointed the mistake. She then asked, "How do you explain this lapse?" Everyone present there was shocked at this rudeness. They anxiously waited for Dr. Johnson's reply.

■ QUESTIONS

1. What was Dr. Johnson's reply?

2. What is the implication of this story?

■ ANSWERS

1. Dr. Johnson coolly replied: "Ignorance, Madam, pure ignorance. Kindly accept my humble apology."

2. Dr. Johnson's humility is admirable. The first test of a great person is his humility. A humble person accepts the possibility of making a mistake due to his limitations. He does not feel insulted to acknowledge that what is known to him is very little, and what is yet to be learnt is immeasurable.

93
Follow the middle path

When the Buddha first embarked upon his spiritual quest, he practised many austerities. The path to spiritual enlightenment was surely not a bed of roses. He believed at that time, that the gateway to spiritualism was through *tapas* (sacrifices) and austerities. To do this, he was too harsh on his own self. One day, he was sitting in deep meditation under a tree. His meditation was disturbed by two musicians talking to each other. One was saying to the other: "Do not tighten too much the strings of your sitar, lest they snap. Nor should you keep them too loose either, otherwise they will produce no music." These words revealed a deep secret to the Buddha and he altered his way of life accordingly.

■ QUESTIONS

1. What did the Buddha learn from the musicians' conversation?

2. What is the implication of this story?

■ ANSWERS

1. Don't go to extremes. Follow a middle path if you want to succeed.

2. Anything done in extreme is bad. Everything done in moderation has greater chances of being implemented right up to the end.

94

Even a crore of rupees can't buy a single second

Once upon a time, there lived a miser who only collected money his entire life, and never ended up spending it. He had accumulated five hundred thousand *dinars,* and looked forward to full year of a lavish lifestyle. But before long, the Angel of Death appeared before him to take him away. The miser begged and pleaded, and used a thousand arguments for some more time on earth, "Give me three days of life and I shall give you half my entire fortune," said the man. The Angel wouldn't hear any of this. "Give me just one day, I beg of you, and you can have everything I accumulated through so much of toil and hard work." The Angel was still adamant.

Then, the man pleaded with the Angel to spare him a few seconds for him to write a note for posterity. The Angel granted him the wish. He wrote the note as follows:

■ QUESTIONS

1. What was the note written by the miser?

2. What is the implication of this story?

■ ANSWERS

1. The Miser's note read: "To whoever you are that happens to find this note, if you have enough to live on, don't waste your life accumulating fortunes. Live! All my five hundred thousand *dinars* couldn't buy me even a single second of my life."

2. The miser's note itself is the message for this story. Death being uncertain for everybody, there is no point in wasting our time only in accumulating wealth beyond a certain limit.

95

Be cautious about what you want

Once upon a time, there was a poor old man who lifted heavy sticks from one place to another for a living. One day, as he was on his way with the heavy load on his back, he grew tired. He sat on the bank of a nearby river and said, "I'm so sick and tired of this. I wish Death would come and relieve me right now." That very moment, Death slipped up from behind, "Here I am. What do you want me to do?" The old man was astonished beyond words.

■ QUESTIONS

1. What did the old man reply?

2. What is the implication of this story?

■ ANSWERS

1. The old man said, "I want you to put this bundle of sticks on my back again."

2. Two things can be derived from this story. One is that

no one really wants to die, unless they commit suicide on the spur of the moment. The second is that whatever we wish for would come to fruition. We must therefore be careful about what we wish for, and must also choose our wishes carefully.

96
Develop practical wisdom

An illiterate cobbler had a bias against educated people. He was once visited by a professor of a college who had only one pair of shoes, and, he asked the cobbler to repair them immediately. "It is closing time," said the cobbler, "It won't be possible for me to repair them just now. Why don't you come for them tomorrow?" "I have only one pair of shoes and I can't walk without shoes."

"Very well, I shall lend you a used pair for the day." "What, and wear someone else's shoes? What do you take me for?"

The cobbler gave the professor an answer that left him speechless.

■ QUESTIONS

1. What was the cobbler's answer?

2. What is the implication of this story?

■ ANSWERS

1. The cobbler said, "Why should you object to having someone else's shoes on your feet, when you don't mind carrying other people's ideas in your head?"

2. Practical wisdom is far superior to bookish knowledge.

97

Learn to use your brain

Awoman was gifted a new electric appliance by her husband. She opened it to realize how complicated the appliance was. With the help of an instruction manual, she tried for hours on end to assemble the complicated thing, but finally gave it up and left all the pieces on her kitchen table. Imagine her surprise, when she got back a few hours later, to find the appliance in a condition ready to use, thanks to her maid servant who did it for her. "How on earth did you do that when you can't even read?" she exclaimed. The maid gave her an answer that left the woman stunned.

■ QUESTIONS

1. What was the maid's reply?

2. What is the implication of this story?

■ ANSWERS

1. The maid said, "Well, Madam, when you don't know how to read, you are forced to use your brains."

2. Everyone is endowed with the faculty of thinking. The so-called illiterates use it abundantly, as they are not able to know the thoughts of others due to lack of literacy. Unconsciously, they develop practical wisdom. At times, even illiteracy can be considered as a blessing in disguise. However, this is not to suggest anyone should remain illiterate.

98
What makes you Holy?

There was a Japanese warrior, who was an ardent disciple of the Buddha. One day, he happened to meet and ask the Buddha, "What makes a person holy?" The Buddha replied, "Every hour is divided into certain minutes and seconds, and every second into certain number of fractions. Anyone who is totally able to be present in each fraction of a second is holy." This Japanese warrior was once captured by the enemies and thrown into prison. At night, he could not sleep for he was convinced that he would be tortured the next morning.

■ QUESTIONS

1. What did the warrior do in the prison to get good sleep?

2. What is the implication of this story?

■ ANSWERS

1. He remembered his Master's words and realized that the only reality that exists in this world is here and

now. So, he came back to the present and fell asleep in a moment.

2. The implication of this story is that the person over whom the past or future have no control is like the bird in the air and the lilies in the field. He experiences freedom and happiness. He does not worry about tomorrow. This total presence in the now is Holiness!

99

Revenge widens the wound

King Henry VIII of England and King Francis I of France were bitter enemies. They were constantly fighting with one another. Once, King Henry requested Sir Thomas More, one of his very learned courtiers, to carry one such sharp note to Francis. More feared that this note would surely have him beheaded in the process. To this, Henry replied, "Not to fear More, if he does that, then I will have the head of every Frenchman in London." In reply, More said, "That's very kind of His Majesty but…."

◼ QUESTIONS

1. What did Sir Thomas More say in reply to the king?

2. What is the implication of this story?

◼ ANSWERS

1. "But I don't think any of the heads will fit my shoulders."

2. Bitterness breeds bitterness.

100
Overcome disabilities

Radhabai became the first blind girl student to get her Ph.D. degree from the Bharathidasan University, Trichy. It took tremendous courage, grit and determination to reach her goal. She said that it was very satisfying to know that she'd reached a big high in life without the use of the most vital sense organ, and especially after the difficulties she had faced on the long road to her achievement.

QUESTIONS

1. What is the implication of the story of Radhabai?

ANSWERS

1. True brilliance shines anywhere. Physical disability cannot be a hindrance to success. Where there is a will, there is always a way out!

101
Develop a magnanimous heart

One day, shortly after Pearl Harbor, Brigadier General Theodore Roosevelt was waiting at an airport to board a plane. Just then, a sailor stepped up to the nearby ticket window, and asked for a seat on the plane. His request was rejected since there was no seat available. He tried to convince the person at the ticket counter saying that he needed to see his mother urgently. But again, his request was rejected on the ground of not being in a position of higher authority. Seeing this, Roosevelt stepped up at the ticket counter and asked the person in charge to give the sailor his own ticket. Captain Sheridan, an American airlines pilot, who was standing there with him asked the General: "Sir, are you not in a hurry to go?" Roosevelt replied.

■ QUESTIONS

1. What did Roosevelt reply?

2. What is the implication of this story?

ANSWERS

1. The General replied: "It's a matter of rank. I am only a General but he is a son."

2. This shows Roosevelt's humane approach, and his deep respect for a son's love for his mother. He considered that visiting the mother is more important for a son than anything else. Such quality of the General made him the President of the country and a much-loved personality.

JAICO PUBLISHING HOUSE
Elevate Your Life. Transform Your World.

ESTABLISHED IN 1946, Jaico Publishing House is home to world-transforming authors such as Sri Sri Paramahansa Yogananda, Osho, The Dalai Lama, Sri Sri Ravi Shankar, Sadhguru, Robin Sharma, Deepak Chopra, Jack Canfield, Eknath Easwaran, Devdutt Pattanaik, Khushwant Singh, John Maxwell, Brian Tracy and Stephen Hawking.

Our late founder Mr. Jaman Shah first established Jaico as a book distribution company. Sensing that independence was around the corner, he aptly named his company Jaico ('Jai' means victory in Hindi). In order to service the significant demand for affordable books in a developing nation, Mr. Shah initiated Jaico's own publications. Jaico was India's first publisher of paperback books in the English language.

While self-help, religion and philosophy, mind/body/spirit, and business titles form the cornerstone of our non-fiction list, we publish an exciting range of travel, current affairs, biography, and popular science books as well. Our renewed focus on popular fiction is evident in our new titles by a host of fresh young talent from India and abroad. Jaico's recently established Translations Division translates selected English content into nine regional languages.

Jaico's Higher Education Division (HED) is recognized for its student-friendly textbooks in Business Management and Engineering which are in use countrywide.

In addition to being a publisher and distributor of its own titles, Jaico is a major national distributor of books of leading international and Indian publishers. With its headquarters in Mumbai, Jaico has branches and sales offices in Ahmedabad, Bangalore, Bhopal, Bhubaneswar, Chennai, Delhi, Hyderabad, Kolkata and Lucknow.

SINCE 1946